breaking through:
Catholic Women Speak for Themselves

breaking
through

Catholic Women Speak for Themselves

Helen M. Alvaré, editor

Our Sunday Visitor Publishing Division
Our Sunday Visitor, Inc.
Huntington, IN 46750

Dedication

To Louis J. Alvaré, 1925-2011

Table of Contents

Introduction

Helen M. Alvaré

So I'm sitting in the chair at the hair salon getting my hair cut by a stylist I've known for a long time, when his friend walks in and sits beside us. My stylist brags to his friend: "Helen here just came back from Pope Benedict's first Mass. She went over as part of the U.S. delegation." His friend doesn't miss a beat: "I'm so sorry," he says. "I hear this guy is terrible on the whole woman thing." I *do* miss a beat, but then I'm ready: "Wow," I say in a dangerously silky voice, "you're amazing." The friend is not getting it. "What?" he replies. I repeat, "You're amazing. I don't know three people who have read everything Pope Benedict has said about women, but apparently *you* have...."

All right, so this isn't the nicest way to make a point. But it has the virtue of being true. Vast numbers of people have made up their minds about all sorts of things pertaining to the Catholic Church without reading or listening to actual Catholic sources. This is ridiculously true when the subject turns to women in the Catholic Church. Observers can't seem to decide whether Catholic women are mouthpieces for a celibate male hierarchy, unthinkingly clinging to home and hearth, or card-carrying feminists who, if they knew what was good for them, would leave the Church, shaking its ancient dust off their sneakers, or pumps, or whatever-the-hell shoes they felt like wearing that day.

On the positive side, the amount of ink devoted to Catholic women indicates that we are doing something possibly fascinating and likely countercultural. Peggy Noonan, writing about the avalanche of press attention to the death of Pope John Paul II, observed a similar phenomenon. Everyone, she wrote, seemed to feel entitled to express an opinion about Pope John Paul, as if he were some kind of public property. She found this reassuring, confirming the Catholic Church's claim and call to be "catholic"/universal. Apparently the public — even if only dimly — perceives this.

The same is apparently true regarding the Catholic woman. Maybe it's because our Church still boasts thousands of women who take vows of poverty, chastity, and obedience — and *like* it. Maybe it's our long (pre-feminist) tradition of women running major institutions such as universities, hospitals, and social services — and doing it without a lot of blather about "striking blows" for women's equality. Their focus has rather been in the nature of "servant leadership" and serving the least among us. Maybe it's because one is just as likely to see a Catholic woman praying at a nuclear-test site or a prison as at an abortion facility, or to see her working at a university as in her home or her own business. Undoubtedly it is due in part to so many Catholic women's refusals to buckle under the reigning ideology that the sexual revolution — particularly its divorcing of sex from babies — is an unmitigated good, or even the *sine qua non* of women's equality. This, in particular, seems to drive a lot of people crazy.

On this last point, divorcing of sex from babies, the Catholic stance has come under a microscope recently due to the federal government's order to religious institutions (with a few exceptions) to provide for their employees' health insurance that covers contraception, sterilization, and drugs that can act as abortifacients. Catholic opposition to this mandate unleashed a recent flood of public and political opinions about whether it makes sense for Catholic women to stick with the Church. Immediately, some female members of Congress asserted that this was a girls-versus-celibate-guys matter. Never one to resist a good ole gender war, leading media jumped in, most capitalizing on the claimed "98 percent" of Catholic women who disagree with Church teaching on birth control (a figure later proved to be sloppily calculated, although the number is undoubtedly very high). At about the same time, a secularist group commissioned an advertisement in the *The New York Times*, responding to Catholic resistance to the Health and Human Services mandate and headlined "It's Time to Consider Quitting the Catholic Church." It asked Catholics: "Will it be reproductive freedom or back to the Dark Ages? Do you choose women and their rights, or bishops and their wrongs?" (March 9, 2012) In short, it doesn't take a rocket scientist to conclude that Catholic teachings about human sexuality are particularly provoking.

On the negative side of this fascination, the press covers the subject of Catholic women largely through the figures and voices of people who refuse to credit our countercultural teachings on sex. Or via those who believe that the faith should really stay in the four walls of a church, or in the space between our mouths and the crucifixes hanging on our walls at home. The former — those media figures who explicitly reject Catholic teachings — are more than a little prone to distort these teachings and attribute nefarious motivations to any male hierarchy who dares to articulate them. The latter — those who believe religion to be a purely private matter —

are anxious to avoid any whisper of Catholic teachings in the public square or even in Catholic institutions which happen to hire and serve non-Catholics as well.

"So the Church Hates Women, Right?"

Presently, America is flirting with the idea of ending its dialogue with, and reliance upon, religion as a credible, trusted source of wisdom and values in the wider society. Catholic institutions have become a particular target. Driving this, in no small part, is the idea that religion is out of step with "freedom," especially women's. (An attorney I debated from the vociferously pro-legal-abortion Center for Reproductive Law and Policy opined that "voices like ours" should not be heard any longer in the public square.) Catholic women in agreement with this perspective get ample media play. The rest of us have to create our own opportunities. Thus this book.

If you want to know who believing Catholic women are, and what we think about being Catholic and female today in connection with a host of hot-button issues, listen to engaged Catholic women, not commentators with little genuine curiosity. Listen to women who are honestly trying to grapple with how their faith might inform their thinking and their acting. Let Catholic women speak for themselves.

Of course, like women in general, Catholic women are not univocal. The women in this book differ not only in age and occupation, but also in socioeconomic and educational background. They tend away from assertions about "all women" or "no women" thinking or doing this or that. Furthermore, they avoid "triumphalism" in favor of humility. They share how, by taking their faith seriously — by reading, praying, thinking, and talking things over with women and men they respect (who are often further along in their spiritual lives) they came to some wisdom. Not all the wisdom there is … but some. They also share their exploration of different possible paths — secular feminism, careerism, materialism, scientism, individualism, and so forth — but how, in the end, they came to the same conclusion as a famous apostle: "Lord, to whom can we go? You have the words of eternal life" (Jn 6:68).

In this book, nine Catholic women are asking themselves the questions we thought you might be asking too. Questions about the times you live in and about the faith. How did I determine the questions? Certainly I scanned leading headlines. I also thought about the questions I get from reporters almost weekly and the questions posed to me during my travels around the United States. A lot of questions emerged from women who had signed an open letter I drafted in concert with friend and fellow author Kim Daniels (Chapter Ten) in response to the claim that there were no women standing with the Catholic Church's demands for religious freedom in opposition to the "contraception mandate" issued by the Obama administration in early 2012. (That letter, signed as of this writing by over 30,000 women, can be found at womenspeakforthemselves.com.)

Freedom and Other "Women's Issues"

Thinking about all of this, it seemed to me that many people want to understand "what freedom looks like" for women today, and how Catholic women in particular understand freedom. There are some very new situations facing women, situations for which there are virtually no historical precedents to guide us. How do we respond to these situations?

The authors in this book have been turning just these kinds of questions over in their minds for a long time. They can't seem to stop asking themselves what freedom means in connection with the Church's teachings on contraception, for example, or on children, or on same-sex marriage. They have been challenged to explain how women's freedom is co-incident with the vowed religious life or dedicated service to one's local parish or neighborhood, especially given the way late twentieth-century feminism gave "service" by women a bad name.

Other authors have felt personally challenged to harmonize their faith with some of the very new questions and situations facing women today. The sex, dating, and marriage market in which younger women live today, for example, is a market shaped in large part by the separation of sex and children, made possible by modern birth control technology and legal abortion. How do Catholic women respond to that?

Others have experienced the lure of materialism and the phenomenon of the female breadwinner brought to us via women's successes in both education and employment over the last few decades. Single motherhood is also a fact of life for more and more women: Today more than 40 percent of all children born annually in the United States are born outside of a marriage. Catholic women have experienced this. What are some possible reflections? Finally, given the rhetoric about the "failure" of the celibate male priesthood in light of the clergy sex abuse scandal, how does a Catholic woman think simultaneously about that scandal and her faith?

This timely book is designed to showcase the ways that some Catholic women have drawn upon the resources of their ancient faith to face completely modern situations. You will see sometimes that the authors have explicit and well-communicated Church teaching to rely upon. Other times they do not. Consequently they are often faced with confronting historically new circumstances as best they can, with the aid of their faith, with prayer, their best understanding of whatever guideposts they can find in Catholic teaching, and the example of loving and more spiritually mature role models.

All of the contributors are Catholic women who have struggled, successfully and with integrity, to figure out how the demands of their faith allow them to live freely and even with joy in the context of some very pointed and current challenges. Their stories and reflections — told in everyday language — should help clear up some of the mystery surrounding Catholic women's continued attraction to their faith and demonstrate what they might bring to American culture.

Loving in Truth

While the stories and thinking in this book are as varied as the women who contributed, you might also discern an underlying theme. I would call that theme "love in truth." Honestly, I do not mean here simply to copy Pope Benedict XVI's 2009 encyclical by the same name, *Caritas in Veritate* ("Love in Truth"). I just believe he was onto something, that he was reading the signs of the times correctly.

Women looking for happiness and freedom are searching for ways to live that might genuinely deserve the name *loving*. But we live in a world that has regularly adulterated the meaning of the word: loving as taking care of number one; loving as sexual license; loving as doing what is emotionally satisfying; loving as never judging; and loving as avoiding suffering. We are, rather, looking for love that will bring genuine goodness, wholeness, happiness, and a spirit of generosity — in a word, love in truth. Love that actually allows us to be the person God meant us to be, and loving that reflects the way we would want to be loved ourselves, the way God loves us.

Developing the capacity to love this way is the work of a lifetime and involves grappling with all the questions raised in this book and with others that space does not permit me to cover all at once. The Church — families, scholars, holy women and men, priests and laypeople — has been thinking about these questions for thousands of years. There is wisdom; there is truth there. But to make progress in each of our lives, it is not sufficient to point to what others have accomplished in the past. Pope Benedict in *Caritas in Veritate* (see Nos. 11, 23, 24, 70) and in *Spe Salvi* ("In Hope We Were Saved," No. 24) reminds us (brilliantly, I might add) that progress in personal goodness and real freedom does not follow the same path as progress in technology, where each successive explorer can build upon what others accomplished before. When it comes to goodness, and freedom, and becoming a loving person on an individual level, each woman and man must begin at the beginning, and build from the ground up.

Another aspect of this book's theme of love in truth concerns the *way* to succeed at loving in truth. That way is to "find oneself by making a sincere gift of oneself." It was a favorite theme of Blessed Pope John Paul II and remains a favorite of Pope Benedict XVI. This is not a way of living that necessarily comes naturally or easily to us. The Scond Vatican Council's document on the Church in the modern world (*Gaudium et Spes*) says that reason alone is insufficient for grasping this truth. Rather, we have to open our minds and hearts to "vistas closed to human reason" (No. 24). We have to open ourselves to grace and to the wisdom that comes from above.

I believe the essays in this book will help you open your mind and heart to these vistas. Certainly, in my own life, in my own experiences traveling nearly every state (hey Wyoming, you never call, you never write…) and many, many countries, I have seen numerous good people who have done just that. I have tried to learn from them.

There was the pro-life director who told me the story of her husband who was building his much longed for "man-cave" in the basement at about the time his last child, a daughter, was scheduled to begin college. He learned that she was pregnant when his wife approached him during construction, carrying in her hand a pack of prenatal vitamins bearing his daughter's name on the prescription. At that instant, he turned around and began tearing down the walls he had just erected. "Honey, it will be all right!" the panicked wife called out. "What are you doing?" "I'm building a *&^%ing nursery," he replied. And he did, and went on to help care for that child every week while his daughter attended college between weekends home.

There was also the married couple in my own parish who agreed without a backward glance to adopt the child of a pregnant woman who was deeply fearful of giving birth to a baby who would be "born dying." The wife had met the pregnant mother while praying outside an abortion clinic and, without even a call home to her husband, offered to adopt the baby. After a year of round-the-clock care in their living room for a child never long removed from medical equipment, Christian died. The wake and funeral of that child were a combination of loss and celebration of life the likes of which I have never seen: the photos displayed of the smiling adoptive parents, their friends and neighbors and extended family, holding Christian and feeding him; the now deceased child, dressed in a tiny, beautiful suit, a look of complete peace and sweetness on his face

In my life and work, I can honestly say that I've experienced hundreds of these stunning moments. One by one, they called out to me to take the lesson: decide to love; decide to give; try mightily to learn the truth; then leap. It is my outsized hope that the stories offered by the women in this book will help you to understand that there is abundant life and freedom on this path.

Chapter 1

Fear of Children

Helen M. Alvaré, J.D., M.A.

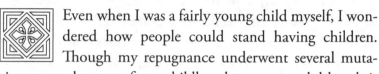Even when I was a fairly young child myself, I wondered how people could stand having children. Though my repugnance underwent several mutations over the years from childhood to young adulthood, it remained essentially fixed. At first it stemmed from a fundamental pessimism about life in this world, a consciousness that life is hard for human beings. This was undoubtedly related to the difficulties my nearest-in-age and disabled sister endured while we were children together. These made me wonder why people would bring innocent beings into the world to suffer its regular disappointments and worse. Childrearing also seemed a truly high-wire business: So much could go wrong. Why risk it?

Only slightly later, as an adolescent and young adult under feminist influence, I began to question why adults, women in particular — with the whole world potentially at their feet — would forego the opportunity to do really interesting things in order, for example, to hang out at the pool every day in the summer, or to cook and clean up after meals, day in and day out. I was pretty well known in my extended family and among my friends for my distaste for the whole business of parenting. I once "famously" told my mother (after discovering some of her impressive college accomplishments) that she "could have *been* something." My second-oldest nephew had a little singsong when he was a toddler that went: "Mommy loves me, Daddy loves me, Aunt Helen doesn't love me...."

Today, however, I stand before you a woman convinced that children *made* me, in the sense of rendering me the halfway decent person I can claim to be. I also know that without them, I would be bored to tears by life in this world. They make me laugh every day and give me 100 reasons to be interested in the goings-on in the world around me. Without them, I am fairly sure that even given my multiple statuses of wife, daughter, sister, friend, and professor, I would have devolved into an even more selfish person than I am. I would also, undoubtedly, be even less patient. Instead, I have learned to grit my teeth and sit through board games, hours of basic math review, and sundry insipid kids' movies without losing my (freaking) mind. I can spend the vast majority of my income on things like kids' schooling, food, clothing, and transportation, and drive a seventeen-year-old truck and a seven-year-old van, and not only remain firm in the conclusion that my priorities are rightly ordered, but *like* the way I live. I can cry about and pray over the losses and reversals of friends and neighbors because I have learned to enter more genuinely into the sufferings of people other than my own little self. And I can see qualities in my husband — unselfishness, determination, wise planning — I would not likely otherwise have seen. Having boys in particular has helped this feminist grasp the charms of males *qua* males. (A friend and I recently laughed to discover that we had both told our husbands how much we had learned to love about men by raising sons, and how useful it would have been to have raised the boys first, and *then* met their fathers.)

I don't mean to imply that children are some sort of utilitarian means to the end of ensuring that I do not go to hell. I believe they may just do that, although I swear I didn't know about their salvific qualities before I had them. But it's true, and I don't think its harmful in any way to tell you that they are indeed a boon to their parents' struggle for goodness, for holiness even, and for learning to put up with other human beings who — amazingly enough — are someone's children too.

My journey from "Aunt Helen doesn't love me" to "children made me" is likely unique, as will be your journey. But it is also quite possible that my journey and yours have common moments too. We are swimming in the same American cultural and economic soup, with some of the same messages coming at us about the meaning of maternity, the contents of the good life, and the practical work involved in rearing children. How could we not worry about one or two of the same things? Further, my conversations with young women and with mothers around the country over the last twenty years have confirmed this intuition.

My first concrete thoughts about the value of children arose in response to the cruelty shown to my (now late) disabled sister in the suburban neighborhood where we grew up. Due to an accident at her birth, she was born — four years before me — with traumatic injuries to her brain. She was the fourth, and I the last, of the children in our family. During the 1960s, it seemed there was a great deal of pressure on the parents of disabled children to grit their teeth and bear privately all the work and worries associated with rearing a disabled child. It wasn't only that there were fewer public and private resources available to guide the families of disabled children. There was also an unspoken expectation that the parents would try to ensure that, outwardly, the child could conform to social standards for "normal" children to the greatest degree possible. Generally, I'm a fan of external standards calling people to expectations loftier than they might otherwise observe. But not meaningless or ultimately harmful standards such as those applied to my sister concerning the emotional maturity, academic prowess, and fashion sense of a disabled girl-child.

My parents worked tirelessly, but it didn't stop the children in my neighborhood from excluding my sister from their play or from ridiculing her appearance, her physical awkwardness, or her emotional neediness. Their parents seemed little better. I have one particularly horrid memory of bursting into the house of my least favorite neighbors during a dinner party and calling the mother out in the presence of all of her guests for her nasty treatment of my sister. Ugh. While I have come to believe that this steeled me for my later public advocacy on behalf of vulnerable unborn children, it still made for a dark Saturday night for a ten-year-old and the victim.

At that time of my life, then, I promised myself I would never have children. Why re-create a *Lord of the Flies* society? Children were too primitive, too selfish, too driven by the desire to be accepted by their peers. And their parents, too, seemed unable to cope with the less-than-perfect children of others. What of the children I knew who didn't fit that mold (and I liked to count myself among them, along with a few of my school friends)? I believed we were few and would always be at the mercy of these others who were the prettiest and most popular kids in the neighborhood. I don't know how my parents' hearts failed to break during those years of my sister's childhood. But I knew I couldn't bear such a large part of life — my own children's happiness — being so utterly out of my control. As I emerged into my late teen years, this sense then merged with a new observation: Times were changing drastically for women in the later 1970s, and it would be easy for me — in fact vastly superior — to avoid motherhood completely. All those boring maternal duties and all the anguish over children's suffering could simply be sidestepped while I made a life out of one of the many interesting possibilities opening up for women in the world.

Enter the Revolution

It is hard to overstate how completely — culturally speaking — my adolescence and early adulthood corresponded with an extremely active phase of American feminism. *Ms. Magazine* was launched in 1971. Congress passed the Equal Rights Amendment in 1972 (although it ultimately failed to be ratified by enough states). Legislation and judicial opinions issued under the banner of "women's equality" and concerning education, abortion, marital rape, access to credit and employment, and so on cascaded onto the scene throughout the 1970s. The sexual revolution was in full swing, promising to alter women's sexual lives and social norms so that these corresponded with the so-called male norm. This claimed norm? Nonmarital sex with no commitment, no shame, and definitely no babies.

Despite my parents' best efforts to keep the revolution out of our traditional Catholic home, it walked right in. Every week when I picked up *Time* magazine, loose pages fell onto the floor because my mother had ripped out their opposite sides for their crime of reporting on the aforesaid sexual revolution. Of course, I just read the excised pages at the local library. Their message was clear: Motherhood was a waste of time, economically worthless, socially disvalued, and particularly so by comparison with the many other paths opening up for women. I felt personally challenged: These were paths that only men had previously taken, paths that paid real money. For self-worth, for income, for excitement, and for real equality, there was nothing like the workplace. That's where the then-reigning gender was, and it was an important source of its power. That's where I thought I should go too.

So-o-o-o, I attended college at a place relatively recently opened to women. Its athletic programs and student activity funding reflected this perfectly. Funding was skewed toward men's social groups and men's athletics. I protested (unsuccessfully) the expenditures for new Astroturf for the football field and petitioned (successfully) to equalize the funding between my women's singing group and the men's. Simultaneously, I began to reflect, both during college and thereafter at law school, that it made no earthly sense to be investing so much in building up my — or any woman's — human capital, and then to abandon it or give it away by failing to exploit it in the workplace.

Now, at this point, some readers are shaking their heads over my gullibility, my wholesale swallowing of the feminist propositions of the late twentieth century. I won't justify it, but there are explanations. Of course, I could have instead learned to appreciate the example shown by my loving parents and my large extended family. My parents cared for us, particularly for my disabled sister, and for our frail elderly grandmother who lived with us until her death. I could have rejected the materialism inherent in a careerist worldview. But the loudest voices in the world were urging women to look elsewhere.

It did not really occur to parents in those days, or even to the religious sisters who taught at my high school, to have an extended conversation with a young woman about the goods of marriage and family or the possibility of making contributions to the world through work both inside and outside the home. It was all too new. Concepts such as "balancing," "flex time," "sequencing," "job sharing," "maternity leave," and "family-friendly employer" hadn't yet been invented. All I could see was that a girl who did well in school and was living in an economy where all things were opening up to women could choose the path marked "excitement" and "success," versus the one labeled "stay home and have kids." Combine this with my *Lord of the Flies* neighborhood and, dear reader, I succumbed.

My story, sans the personal distaste for children, was certainly playing out in America in general beginning at that time. Consequently, from the 1970s to today, birth rates have declined and abortion rates have risen. The "mommy wars" are alive and kicking as women continue to argue over the relative value of work inside versus outside the home.

Also, it is probably fair to say that still today the legal and cultural "toolkit" for women trying to handle mothering and some amount of paid work is still quite small. It is not at all sufficient for the way families live in our modern economy. There is no requirement that employers pay a "family wage" so that one parent could stay home during the early years or to care for a sick child or parent. Jobs that pay a lot of income to one spouse usually result in a lot "less spouse" at home.

They also tend to be located in parts of the country where it is expensive to live. People who want to send their children to religious schools are confronted with the relatively high cost of these institutions. And don't even get me started on the costs of college, even lower-cost state colleges. Also, while more jobs can be performed remotely, still, the vast majority of employment requires leaving home to travel to work. Complicating the picture, our economic times have raised real questions about the future supply of work performed traditionally by men — jobs requiring on average greater physical strength — while the supply of work in jobs equally available to both sexes has soared.

A Growing Intuition

Considering all of this, what are the circumstances that led me to children nevertheless? It seems appropriate at this moment to stop and thank God for this thing people often call women's biological clock. In my own case, I could hear it going off even though nothing in my conscious brain had deduced that "it's time" to have children. I didn't suddenly change my response to babies. Today, I have a bad case of "aww, look at that beautiful baby," but no such condition affected me before I had children. Even now, I have trouble putting words to the transformation.

Part of it was a growing consciousness that my husband and I were living for ourselves alone — and in a happy marriage this feels quite similar to living for oneself. Staring down the years together, it seemed problematic to envision ourselves simply continuing to do nothing but entertain ourselves and our friends and feather our nest, even if we were also engaging in volunteer work at times — he regularly donating platelets to a boy with leukemia, and me hanging out at a nursing home near our apartment with a woman who had no family. There just grew in me a sense that there must be more to life, something at that moment closed to my understanding. It also occurred to me that I did not aspire to be like some married people I had met who seemed allergic to children. With almost no exceptions, I did not admire their lives. This gave me pause.

There was also developing in my head the notion that while I knew this man, my husband, well and for years, even before we began dating, I wasn't fully his partner. We lived beside one another beautifully, but still we did not seem integrated enough. It was as if there was something missing in my belonging to him and him to me. I began to think that this might change in the presence of a child who was ours. That this would be a qualitatively different kind of togetherness as distinguished from all of the other things we did together — talk, entertain, read, visit families, commute, shop, and so on. It was that basic an intuition.

There was also this: The Catholic Church seemed always to be going on about how great a gift children are, referring to them by using expressions like the "crown" or "summit" of marriage. All my life, I had been very much a "daughter of the Church," convinced in my mind, and attempting to put into practice in my life, that no one had a better account than she did of the world, and of how people ought to live in it, alone and together, in marriage and in the wider society. This conviction remained true despite my coming into regular contact with people who disagreed with this conclusion, sometimes vehemently. I therefore decided to grant the Church deference and even credence on its point about children. She was wiser and kinder than I, so perhaps I should take a flyer.

I wish I could tell you the transition was easy, that once I had opened my heart and my mind to children all went well. But instead it was pretty darn awful. My pregnancies either ended in miscarriage (more than a few) or were very easy. But the first attempt at parenting was hard, very hard. We struggled with breastfeeding every day for months. Between feeding and "the pump," I spent about six hours a day just getting the minimal amount of food into my first baby. Nine or ten formulas later, we ended up required by a pediatric gastroenterologist to feed her goat milk from a farm where the female and male goats were kept separately so that the milk wouldn't smell awful. (This led to some interesting encounters at the only store selling such milk where, thanks to my husband, I learned to reply to the endless inquiry "Why aren't you breastfeeding" with a mumbled lie: "double mastectomy").

I loved my new baby and saw new and amazing things in this man who had previously been only my husband, but was now also somebody's father. I saw new capabilities in myself too. Still, it would not be accurate to say that I thought of myself in maternal terms. Rather, I was still a woman who did X and Y and Z, but who was also taking care of a baby girl. This was a very demanding job, but not yet a vocation.

Not long after, and without knowing why, my husband I and concluded that *of course* we would not want this child to be an only child. We had no blessed idea why. (The more I review this period of my life, it's clear that some mind better than my own was, in fact, guiding my thoughts and actions about parenting.) It wasn't as if I suffered rose-colored reflections on my life as one of five siblings, or received sage advice from prior generations about the beauties of siblings. I didn't even make the utilitarian calculations about the usefulness of having one child to distract the other, or the good of having more children to take care of us in old age. The most I can say is that we felt called to have a bigger community. To have more life going on around us. And I wanted to join again in such a partnership with the man I loved.

Of course, the next child was an easier adjustment. But what I remember most is the moment when he was just six or seven weeks old, and it occurred to me that I was officially open for more children in a very, very positive way. That I didn't want to count or calculate anymore — I just wanted a family community with more life in it, whatever we could reasonably manage. Why did this happen? Surely, I was a more relaxed parent, thank God. This allowed me to see my baby boy as he was, and not any longer to see only my own incompetence as a parental unit. But there was something else, some new openness to life that had been gifted to me; thus my third-born child, and others later conceived but lost to miscarriages. In particular, I won't forget my being pregnant at age forty-five (ve-e-e-e-ry close to forty-six, if you must know) when I told my husband the news, and he replied without missing a beat, "Well, we've always wanted another girl." And I responded, "Let's just grandparent this baby. Let's just decide not to worry at all about anything," although I was fairly sure that at my advanced age, the child would be born with at least some disability. How times had changed.

Accepting the Gift

So what do I understand now, almost twenty years into this journey? Not a whole lot, but a few things. I understand first that, practically speaking, living for myself — or as a couple living for ourselves — would be a terrible temptation toward materialism, ego, and selfishness. Self-giving to a sacrificial extent is just more likely to happen when it's in your face, in your house, where you get relentless opportunities to rise above your own self-interest, your own weaknesses, and to take care of others for decades, not hours.

I also understand how intensely bored my husband and I would be without all that children have opened us to. And I say this as a person who has been very lucky to have a job that involves constant reading, writing, speaking, and traveling a good chunk of the world to some legendarily cool places. Yet I can still conclude that watching another person develop, and listening to how children react to the world around them, and having the chance to watch them choose to be unselfish, or even generous, and reach out for a relationship with God, is the coolest thing. At a certain point, I remember saying to myself while traipsing around yet another beautiful European capital for work: I would *so* rather be home with my husband and kids.

I now understand my prior thinking about children as my giving in to the temptation to refuse the basic human vocation to love. Bam. I've said it. I was resisting that whole finding-oneself-in-losing-oneself way of life that the last two popes in particular are always talking about. I didn't want to experience the trials associated with the Christian way of life: self-gift, for as long a time as parenting takes. Have children made me truly "good"? Only God can say, but I am sure that I am thereby at least better than I would otherwise have been.

Finally, whereas before I had been convinced that having children would prevent me from using the years of learning and experience I had amassed at school and at work (where would I find the time?), I have come to see that I have good things to share in large part *because* of the ability to love that children have provoked in me. St. Thomas Aquinas was right: "Lord, in my zeal for the love of truth, never let me forget the truth about love." How does this work? In practical terms, of course, one discovers that she can get off the couch at 11 p.m. to pick up a child somewhere, simply because that child needs a ride. One learns that she has the fortitude to pick up an extra job in order to pay for braces or a school trip. Maybe most importantly, however, one learns how to communicate with other people, to decide in advance to give them "that look of love they crave" once you begin to see them as other people's children.

In 2011, I gave a series of lectures to thousands of teen-agers at World Youth Day in Spain. The subject was love, sex, and marriage. A young priest who was present later said to me: "You are knowledgeable about the law and about fam-ily data, I can tell, and that makes you believable. But your speeches seem wise to me, and you can deliver them with a smile, I believe, only because you are a mother who has prac-ticed loving your family for a long time now." Amen to that, Father.

Helen M. Alvaré is a law professor at George Mason University in Arlington, Virginia, where she teaches and writes in the areas of family law, and law and religion. She is also a Senior Fellow at the Witherspoon Institute in Princeton, New Jersey, and Chair of the Task Force on Conscience Protection, as well as a Consultant to the Pontifical Council for the Family. Previously, she was the voice of the U.S. Catholic bishops on matters concerning respect for life, and a litigation associate at a Philadelphia law firm. She is married with three children.

Chapter 2

Contraception
Wrestling with Reality

Marie Anderson, M.D.

 I was raised as a Catholic, but for much of my life, including many years as an obstetrician-gynecologist, I looked at the Church's teachings on contraception and said, "That's impossible! In this day and age, with all the medical advances we have, why would anyone want to deny herself the best modern medicine has to offer? Why would anyone want to give up the right to decide whether and when to become a mother?" I freely prescribed contraceptives and even performed abortions on babies considered too damaged to survive outside the womb. This is the story of how I came to believe that what I once thought was impossible is not only possible, but essential.

Stumbling Toward the Future

As a young girl growing up in a Catholic family in Indiana, I found life complicated. My mother experienced a horrific reproductive life, and I witnessed it firsthand. She suffered one miscarriage after another, a stillbirth at six months, a neonatal death at seven months. Since I was the oldest, I watched as she endured continuous bleeding and what seemed like unending bed rest, all of which ultimately resulted in her hemorrhaging and being taken away by ambulance. What a terrifying thing for a five-year-old to see. At the time, I didn't understand what was happening to my mother. I felt awful because I couldn't help her, and I thought I might never see her again. I was afraid.

As a stark contrast to my complicated home life, I also remember the simplicity of attending Saint Mary's grade school along with most of my friends. Just about everyone I knew was Catholic. All of that changed when my parents decided to transfer to Virginia so my father could fulfill his lifelong dream of raising thoroughbred racehorses. My parents, my two sisters, and I moved to a horse farm. It was a great place to be a child, but it was in a rural area with no access to a Catholic school, and so we attended public school during the week and religious education classes on Sundays. Initially, this arrangement worked well because my mother taught our classes. She soon became pregnant with our youngest sister, however, and could no longer teach because her pregnancy was high-risk.

I came of age during the tumultuous 1960s. The Vietnam War was raging, Betty Friedan's *The Feminine Mystique* challenged notions of what women can and should do, and women everywhere were burning their bras. Feminism came to fruition while I was in high school.

Our religious education classes reflected the times. Our pastor, wanting us to have the best teachers, hired students from a leading Catholic university. Many of them, it turned out, had serious disagreements with the Church. Several dropped out of school, but before they did they spoke their minds about why they were leaving. They taught the faith from a contemporary and political viewpoint rather than according to ancient, well-tested beliefs. No boring dogma for us! We learned to start by questioning everything. They encouraged us to think critically and independently, to form our own conscience, and to act on it — good things in and of themselves, but they gave us no foundation, no solid teaching to guide our thinking.

The times were changing, and they made certain we could change with them. Additionally, there was an anticipation that the Church would rule favorably on this new technology called the pill. I graduated high school having heard these messages. I relied on my own ideas — which I called my "conscience" — without really properly forming my conscience. Not surprisingly, I fell away from my faith shortly after I graduated from high school.

I had always wanted a career in some aspect of medicine, but after two years I transferred from pre-med to dental hygiene, because I didn't want to be in training until I was thirty — which medicine required. I felt that would hinder my ability to marry and have a family. I met my future husband in dental school, and when the time came we married in the Church.

We contracepted, had our two children, and figured our family was complete. Soon, my desire to become a doctor resurfaced. Specifically, I wanted to be an obstetrician-gynecologist not only because of my mother's experiences — I wanted to help women like her — but also because I had become fascinated by the field during my pregnancies. Being an ob-gyn attracted me just as certainly as a magnet attracts metal. My husband supported this decision, and so I started medical school at thirty-five. I still had a childhood faith, but I did nothing to change it. I was stumbling through life aware that faith was critical — I had this feeling in my gut that I had avoided addressing the tough questions — but I continued to procrastinate. I wanted to be like everyone else. I wanted life to be as simple as it was when all of my friends attended the same Catholic grade school with me.

A Pivotal Conversation

I went to a Catholic medical school where I learned many things, including the fact that I was very angry. Thus began the conflicted process of growing in the faith I had ceased to practice. There was a chapel in the medical school, and whenever I walked past it, I was mysteriously drawn to it. It seemed familiar, reminding me of my childhood and my days at Saint Mary's. One day, I walked into the chapel and just sat down with Our Lord, the first of many such visits. Eventually I went to Mass there, and one day after Mass I asked the priest if we could talk. What a talk it was! I poured out such virulent anger that I was astonished. I had no idea where it came from. Eventually it became clear that I was angry at the Church because I felt it was unfair to women. Many times it had been rumored that the Church was considering change on issues particularly pertinent to women, but every time the ancient teachings were not only upheld, they were strengthened. I felt that Church teaching stood in the way of the life I wanted and the schedule I had set for myself to achieve my goals. I was deeply shaped by the feminism of the times, much more than I realized.

I thought the rules were ridiculous. As a woman with a scientific bent, I was appalled that the Church banned what I believed to be some of the best achievements science had to offer. The Church didn't seem to understand that in order to compete in the workplace, for example, women needed to have reliable contraception. I didn't want to be a part of any church that disrespected women the way the Catholic Church seemed to. It was run by men, and it was simply out of date. The priest listened quietly.

I told him about my mother's obstetric disasters and the fear I had experienced as a child. I wanted to cure women like my mother, and I was convinced that the Church's stance on contraception was an obstacle to that. Women like my mother, whose life was literally threatened with each pregnancy, should not have to get pregnant. When I was older, she confided in me that she had used the rhythm method to avoid pregnancy — a very different method from natural family planning, but all that was known at the time. Obviously, that was not effective for my parents. It made me angry to think that Catholic women had to put their lives in danger to practice their faith. I wanted to change that.

At the conclusion of our meeting, the priest told me I was very complex. I wasn't quite certain what that meant, but I knew it wasn't a compliment.

Storm Clouds Gather

My husband balanced our family needs with his busy dental practice as my life became chaotic with classes and homework. I was too busy, as well, to listen to the whispers from God letting me know he was near. I began to feel restless. I didn't know it then, but it would eventually be this restlessness that would help me resolve my issues with the Church. I still attended Mass whenever I could because I felt safe there, and I experienced Christ's love. I simply ignored the things

I didn't like, distancing myself from the tough questions because I wasn't ready to hear the answers.

Near the end of my second year of medical school, I missed my period. I thought it was due to stress, because I had certainly had enough of that. But then I started throwing up. I thought it must be the flu. Then I took a pregnancy test. It was positive. How could that be? I hadn't wanted to become pregnant, and we were contracepting, so the news came as a complete surprise.

I continued the pregnancy, delivered our son, graduated from medical school, and began a residency in ob-gyn. At first everything seemed fine because the program, very in tune with the world, offered what appeared to be reasonable solutions to life's problems. I was pleased to see that a woman really could control her reproductive life. (Somehow I overlooked the fact that contraception had failed me.)

It was during residency, however, that I truly came into contact with evil. But no one else seemed to think anything was wrong, so I convinced myself that I was doing the right things. For example, I had not previously considered what happens when babies are unwanted because they are imperfect or inconvenient. But now I saw women who were pregnant with imperfect babies abort them in order to try again for a better outcome. I also saw women have abortions because their contraception failed, or they were in school, or it was just not the right time to have a child, and then struggle to act as though nothing had happened. I saw anguish in their faces. Many of them developed eating disorders, had flashbacks, or became clinically depressed. Some even suffered from post-traumatic stress disorder, which is similar to what some soldiers develop after being in war.

Whenever a patient delivered her second child, we residents offered her the choice to have her tubes tied — and sometimes pressured her. Our mantra was to "stamp out fertility" — have your two children and move on with life. At a Catholic hospital, we had to pretend we were trying to fix a broken menstrual cycle, rather than breaking a cycle that worked properly, so we wrote "cycle control" on our birth control prescriptions so that they would be approved by the sister who supervised the clinic. In addition to learning about stamping out fertility, I also learned about in-vitro fertilization during my work at an infertility clinic. In sum, what I really learned in residency is that ob-gyn is a field in which men and women often try to play God. I had reservations.

Although I took these things at face value — it's the way of the world, I told myself — in the back of my mind the storm clouds of restlessness were gathering. They were threatening, but I disregarded them, thinking all the while that someday I'll deal with that, but not today. I ignored my questions because I thought there would be no way to practice ob-gyn without doing those things. I began to feel guilty because it seemed that everything we did, with the exception of delivering babies, broke a rule of the Catholic Church. Again and again I questioned why there were so many rules, and why the Church seemed so outdated.

Turning Point

I completed my residency and joined a practice. I told the doctor during my job interview that I was pro-choice, and although I didn't want to perform abortions myself, I believed it was not my place to stop others from doing so. I agreed, though, to terminate the babies who had been deemed incompatible with life. For awhile I accepted that arrangement, but I was never comfortable with it. I began to consider my life's legacy and the contribution I wanted to make. My unanswered questions still hovered like thunderclouds. I could see them if I shut my eyes. They were in my peripheral vision. Not only was I restless, I was uncomfortable — so uncomfortable that I walked into a confessional for the first time in a long time. What happened there was amazing, but it was only a start. I found myself confessing sins that I had denied for years. It was both a relief and a dilemma. I wanted to change what I was doing, but I was afraid I wouldn't be able to do that at my current job. Little did I know then that it would take me two years to resolve my issues.

I began attending Mass regularly on Sunday. One day after Mass, something on the parish bulletin board outside of church caught my eye. It was an article about Dr. John Bruchalski and the Tepeyac Family Center ob-gyn office he had begun in Fairfax, Virginia. It was totally pro-life. They did not do abortions or sterilizations, or prescribe contraception. That was impossible! How could they stay in practice? How could they find patients? How could they withstand the criticism of their peers? God sometimes works miracles by giving us just the right circumstances and the necessary grace. That day, he gave me everything I needed. I looked at Dr. Bruchalski's picture — his gentle and peaceful face — and knew I could relate to him. I began to imagine myself practicing as he practiced. I thought about it for a long time before I walked away from that newspaper article. That was my turning point.

A few days later, a patient of mine wanted an abortion. I didn't refer her for one. My boss called me into her office and asked me why, since it was "obviously" in the patient's best interest. She then asked me if I would help my daughter obtain an abortion under similar circumstances. I said I wouldn't. Two weeks later she fired me on the basis of my contract's "no cause" clause. Someday, she said, I would find the place I was meant to work, but her office wasn't it. I was devastated. Little did I know that she had just done me a huge favor, because she had hastened my journey home.

I returned to the priest who had heard my confession, and I asked many questions. Some he answered, but some he couldn't. He recommended I meet with Dr. Bruchalski. That name again! For many reasons, it took me months to meet with him, but when I finally did I was impressed most of all by his amazing peace. By now I was more than restless, and I desperately wanted what made him so peaceful.

We met several times. Although raised a Catholic, he had worked in an in-vitro fertilization clinic during his residency, performed abortions, and prescribed contraceptives. He had been a pro-choice doctor who went into medicine to help women, but as time passed he began to wonder if his solutions were making women happier and healthier. It didn't seem that way — the more abortions and contraceptives he provided, the more broken relationships, and infections, and sorrow he saw. And he began to consider the humanity of the babies he was aborting. His gradual return to his faith and the realization that Church teaching was based in respect for the human person began with a pilgrimage to Tepeyac Hill in Guadalupe, Mexico City, where, in the sixteenth century, the Blessed Mother had appeared to Juan Diego. He was inspired during that pilgrimage to found a pro-life ob-gyn office, and although it took him a year, he also changed his practices during his residency in order to be in concert with Church teachings. What courage! I wondered how he did that, since I had assumed it was impossible.

Over the next two years I learned that women deserve something better than either contraception or the old rhythm method. That something is natural family planning (NFP). Not only is it 99 percent effective in avoiding pregnancy, but it is also chemical-free, poses no risks to a woman's health, and helps to build communication between husband and wife. Further, as women learn to observe and chart their cycles and collect other information about their reproductive health, they can use NFP to achieve pregnancy, if that is desired, or to work with their doctors to uncover underlying gynecological problems. A woman already has everything she needs to accomplish her fertility goals, and with a little coaching she can learn how to observe fertility signs, correctly interpret them, and act accordingly. As to the periodic abstinence from sex required by those seeking to avoid pregnancy: Couples learn to cherish the periodic reenactment of the engaged abstinence alternating with the exuberance of the honeymoon — and *that* is good for marriage. This almost certainly sounds strange to modern ears, but I have seen it play out too many times to doubt it any longer.

Unfortunately, Dr. Bruchalski's practice was not looking for new physicians. I eventually accepted a job with a Catholic practice that, I soon discovered, was somewhat less than Catholic. Nevertheless it was an improvement over where I had been. Abortions were not allowed unless the baby had been deemed incompatible with life, or one of the new doctors slipped by the watchful eye of the senior partner. We prescribed contraceptives and carried out sterilizations. Soon I was miserable — my Catholic beliefs on one side, and what I was actually doing at work on the other.

The Courage to Change

I continued to see the priest and Dr. Bruchalski. I mustered the courage to quit aborting "incompatible-with-life" babies after one particular incident. I had terminated a woman's pregnancy because her baby had a lethal diagnosis, but when the patient returned for her postpartum check, I couldn't believe what I saw. It was as if her soul had been sucked out of her. She was the personification of unimaginable, unresolved grief. I thought: There must be a better way. In retrospect, I know from my experiences with perinatal hospice that there *is* a better way. That way is to support the mother and pre-born baby throughout the remainder of the pregnancy. We should not be in a hurry to send the baby back to God because it is imperfect. Mothers want to be with their babies, especially when they are sick. While it is sad to lose a child, we can experience a blessed joy in knowing we shared our child's brief life for the time God gave us. I have seen this happen on several occasions, despite the uncertainty and fear some pregnant women have about their ability to do such a thing.

Taking that step helped me to finally admit that IUDs — intrauterine devices — work by an abortifacient effect. I quit IUD placements. I stopped performing sterilizations because the procedure mutilates the human body. All the while I was praying intently. I had never before experienced the love that completely enveloped me and gave me a sense of total well-being, of solace, peace, and courage. I felt God would care for me no matter what happened. I had never felt like that before. When I was in medical school, the priest had told me to be quiet and listen because God speaks to us in silence. Back then, I couldn't sit down and stop talking long enough to find silence, let alone hear anyone whisper to me in it. Later, I realized I couldn't find silence because, while I was seeking it, I expected God to send it to me on demand. Once I stopped looking for it, it found me. He found me. When that finally happened, I knew unmistakably that I had experienced something extraordinary.

During this time one particular problem kept recurring. When I was on call in the middle of the night, it often happened that a woman would arrive in labor. She would be scheduled for a cesarean and tubal ligation sterilization in the future, but meanwhile she had gone into labor and needed to be delivered immediately by cesarean section. The sticking point was always the sterilization. It is a simple procedure to perform while the patient is already open for the cesarean. It is not so simple later, especially because she probably would have developed scars as a result of the cesarean. I was repeatedly pressured to do the tubal, or to step aside just long enough for someone else to do it. It was one of the major reasons I finally quit that job.

The last thing I gave up was contraception. Not only did my re-found faith tell me to stop, but I also began to look more critically at the medical literature. I discovered remarkable things that I had previously overlooked or refused to see. The pill was not as safe as I had once thought. Journal articles warned about pill users having a higher rate of large, life-threatening blood clots called deep vein thrombosis (DVT).

Hypertension was more common in pill users. A number of studies reported an increase in heart attacks and strokes, especially with higher-dose pills. There was an increased risk of adenocarcinoma, a particular type of cervical cancer, in oral contraceptive users. Benign liver tumors were more common, as were harmful metabolic effects for people such as diabetics. These problems were real — and there were many others, and with other methods as well. (Quite recently, for example, a flurry of studies is showing possible links between hormonal contraceptives such as Depo-Provera and increased susceptibility to HIV infection.)

I remembered, too, the side effects I had personally experienced on the pill: nausea, constant headaches, weight gain, dysfunctional bleeding, mood changes. In listening to my patients, I found most of them had also experienced these symptoms. And since no contraceptive fully protects against sexually transmitted diseases, I also saw women with STDs, many of which resulted in damage that led to infertility. But what was most damning was not the physical impact, but rather the emotional impact that I was seeing day after day among so many of my patients. Far from freeing women, the pill and other contraceptives allowed them to be used as objects of sexual entertainment and allowed both men and women to separate sex from commitment. I felt that, in some significant way, women were breaking their own hearts. At this point, I had long since believed that contraception was wrong. Now the scientific literature raised health concerns. I could no longer deny the truth.

To stop prescribing contraception often results in a mismatch between patients who want contraception and a doctor who won't prescribe it. It essentially means the doctor must start or join another practice composed of patients who are open to natural family planning. I decided to no longer prescribe contraceptives, but that left me with quite a dilemma: I had already assumed, probably because of my pessimistic attitude, that it would be impossible to stop and remain in my current practice.

I kept thinking about the Tepeyac Family Center, however, where they not only avoided prescribing contraception, but they taught and supported NFP, assisted women in crisis pregnancies, and also served the poor. In short, many wonderful things were happening there. It had been essential that I see that role model — I needed reassurance that living according to two thousand years of Church teachings is a reasonable thing to do. And so one day I made the choice and went a full day in the office without prescribing contraceptives. I was so excited that afterward I called a friend who was aware of my struggles with contraception, but unaware that I was ready to take the step. She gasped and told me that, though she had said nothing to me about it, she had been praying a novena for me, and that it had concluded that day. A novena is a prayer prayed consecutively for nine days in order to obtain some special favor. Often, the praying person asks a particular saint to intercede on his or her behalf. This novena was through the intercession of Saint Rita of Cascia who is, like Saint Jude, a patron saint of the impossible, and that day, unbeknownst to me, was her feast day.

This is only one of many events that led me back to my faith. I suddenly was remarkably confident that I had found the truth. It was a slow process, but by asking the questions, considering the impact of my actions on the women I served, and facing the realities of the medical and psychological and cultural consequences of contraceptive use and abortion,

I could see the great wisdom in the Church's teachings. Far from harming women, including women like my mother, the Church was willing to ask hard questions about the meaning of human life, and to look for solutions to medical and cultural problems that did not violate the dignity of women or harm the most vulnerable among us, the child in the womb. Particularly respecting women in my mother's situation, I came to understand so much more. That the Church was not asking each woman to have as many children as physically possible, but only, in its own words, for "responsible" childbearing. That natural family planning was different and vastly superior as a fertility-comprehension method as compared with the rhythm method. And that it was not for me to question my mother's decision regarding how to be a faithful Catholic woman, or to question God's design for every single human life, whether its way of suffering or its way of joy. The Church had been right all along. No longer did I care what people thought of me, or what the consequences might be. At last I was living my faith, even at work. I cannot begin to describe what a blessing and a relief that was. It was life-changing.

It became obvious to me that God knew I existed and cared about me. He made a connection with me, speaking to me through certain events in my life that wouldn't usually have unfolded the way they did. Maybe they were happenstance, maybe not. I'm convinced they were miracles because, for one thing, my prayer life became more bountiful than I could ever have imagined. There was a supernatural element that had never previously been there, which I couldn't explain.

The most amazing thing was that for the first time in my life, I believed the truth. And that's not all. I finally realized that in the past, when I was making major faith decisions with regard to my practice of ob-gyn, I was doing so with a child's faith. I chose ob-gyn because I wanted to heal women. God gently guided me to learn that while I *treat* women, it is God who *heals* them according to his plan.

Eventually, I took a position with Tepeyac Family Center because I wanted to do more than just avoid harmful practices; I also wanted to make a positive contribution. I wanted to care for women of similar faith, support NFP, counsel women experiencing a crisis pregnancy, and help women whose babies had a terminal diagnosis. There was so much I hoped to contribute. I joined Tepeyac almost fifteen years ago, and I have never once regretted my decision.

In retrospect, I am amused that the very field I chose with an attitude of defiance toward God is the very field he used to draw me closer to my faith and help me find the truth.

Whatever you think of the Church's stance on contraception — whether you accept it, or you have misgivings about limiting access to it — you owe it to yourself to prayerfully search for the truth. Then dare to believe it and act on it. Remember, all things are possible with God's help, even giving up contraception and being at peace with that decision.

Dr. Marie Anderson is an obstetrician-gynecologist and medical director of the Tepeyac Family Center in Fairfax, Virginia, where she has practiced for fifteen years. She is also a member of the INOVA Fair Oaks Hospital Ethics Committee and president of the Northern Virginia Guild of the Catholic Medical Association. She is married with three children, one of whom is deceased.

Chapter 3

Sex, Mating, and the Marriage "Market"

Elise Italiano, M.A.

In the time it takes to load her groceries in her shopping cart, the single woman can learn from an array of magazines that if she uses birth control her complexion will be radiant, that cleavage is an essential part of her day-to-evening wardrobe, that there are 537 new ways to please her man, and that if said man is a different man each night of the week, she can be considered more sexually "mature." Perhaps the Bible for the single woman of today is *Sex and the City*. Though aspects of this show are obviously exaggerated, it is natural for the single woman to focus on what she does see there that is appealing: success in a career; regular, frequent opportunities for dating; and enviable wardrobes. It is also easy to feel camaraderie with women such as Carrie, Miranda, Samantha, and Charlotte when they are navigating the questions asked by single women everywhere: How do I know if he cares for me? What circumstances should prompt me to make sacrifices for my career or in my personal life? What does it mean to be a loyal friend to my girlfriends? And the perennial question: Can men and women be friends?

Despite the similarities, though, the Catholic woman can only view the world using Carrie's lens for so long. The questions I wrestle with regarding who I am, what I desire, and what I hope for, overlap with Carrie only insofar as we are both single, heterosexual women hoping for real and lasting companionship. But single, Catholic women need to contend also with questions about vocation, discipleship, practicing virtue, and understanding femininity as both a gift and responsibility. In the end, my questions as a single, *Catholic* woman might go something like this if articulated in Carrie's style:

> I couldn't help but wonder … if tolerance is our highest societal virtue, when will my lifestyle as a woman committed to chastity, monogamy, the sanctity of every human life, to social justice, and obedience to religious authority be accepted as an empowered way of living? When will society take seriously my views of healthy sexual relationships, the measure of success in a career, and the promotion of the value of women?

Plenty of Catholic women are asking themselves the same questions, and more will be doing so as they begin to rethink the implications of the sexual revolution. It's time to allow Catholic women to join the conversation about the changing topography of the relationship and marriage market.

It seems to me that part of the reason that Catholic women are ostracized from the cultural conversation is that they have been completely misunderstood, or at best, shallowly understood. Our identities, particularly as sexual beings, are largely ignored. The thing is, while it might have been easier to disregard Catholic voices in previous generations, my generation is creating a vocal presence in the virtual world and in the public square that must be taken seriously.

So, who are these women? What does their experience look like? I hope that both the culture and the Church will benefit from a description of some of our dating and relationship experiences.

Modern, Catholic, and Misunderstood

My generation is big on self-identity. We build Facebook profiles detailing the aspects of our lives we want to make public. People know what we like, what we are thinking at any given moment, and with whom we spent any given Saturday night. We make online dating profiles to list nonnegotiable traits in a partner and things about ourselves that potential spouses need to know before they broach a first date. We paint our self-portraits for the public to see, and we hope that someone will "like" what we post or make a positive comment about what we've revealed. Why this cultural phenomenon has emerged is beyond the scope of this chapter, but my generation finds a great deal of satisfaction and peace in the affirmation of our identities.

Though I do not fully subscribe to this idea of projecting an identity and seeking affirmation, I do find some merits in describing who I am, both as a member of the Church and as a modern woman in the world. I am a single, dating, practicing Roman Catholic woman in her late twenties who subscribes to *Magnificat* and *Real Simple*, who bookmarks *instyle.com* in addition to the Vatican news site. I listen to Bruce Springsteen and Gregorian chant. I like to do both cardio exercises and Ignatian exercises. In a nutshell, as a woman committed to her faith and one who believes that our culture is not yet a total moral dystopia, I often find that I belong to neither world — mine is an identity that the secular world and the Church seem unable to affirm at this point in history. In my view, the identity of the single, Catholic woman is misunderstood and misrepresented in both spheres. But the love of culture and the love of the Church impel me to describe the hopes, fears, and joys of this state of life in order to make clear to the editors of *Glamour* and my pastors alike what I need, who I am, and who I am not. I do not intend to speak on behalf of anyone else's experience, although I suspect that Catholic women share similar stories and that non-Catholic women might find something worthwhile here.

This Isn't Your Mother's Experience

Single Catholic women live in a world that is far different from the world of our mothers. My own mother's questions about marriage and her role as a woman in the world were answered earlier than mine. By twenty-two she had graduated from college, gotten a job, and married my father. Soon after, they became parents, and together she and he worked out questions about our family, my mother's vocation in and out of the home, and where to put down roots. As I see it, as a woman living during a time of significant social change, she could count success in the eyes of her peers by receiving a university education and getting a career, and she fit rather easily into the life of her parish as a young wife and mother.

Though I have no doubt she navigated her own set of questions about her femininity, mine vary significantly from hers. At twenty-two, like my mother, I had graduated from college ... and this is where our paths diverge. I would wonder not when I would get married, but *if* I would get married. As the tenure of my single life outstripped my mother's by quite a few years, I found myself facing questions she didn't have to face. I wouldn't think about family vacations or dinner parties; instead, I'd wrestle with the fact that my peers were continuing to have social lives mirroring those they had in college: frequenting bars and clubs, drinking to excess, and hooking up — meaning anything from kissing to having sex — with a wider pool of people. I would wrestle with whether or not to put off graduate school or career pursuits in the hope that Mr. Right would come along. I had the opportunity to move wherever I wanted in the world and to do whatever I wanted, all while struggling with a desire to belong somewhere. The most glaring discrepancies I've found between her experience and mine as a woman have been in the arena of dating, mating, and marriage. Quite frankly, it seems like those worlds could not be more different.

Dating and "Sexpectations"

The dating scene has long been compared to a playing field. This analogy probably worked well in my mother's generation. It seems from her stories that the general pattern was to casually date until a relationship turned into something more serious. There was clear meaning behind certain actions. A woman probably dated more locally than globally, meaning that she had certain shared worldviews and experiences to draw from. Moreover, she likely had fewer choices, and so she focused not on finding a perfect match, but on finding a good match with whom she could work toward something better than the sum of its parts.

Today though, if we still call dating a game, then it is one without rules and clear guidelines, one in which the luxuries of time and choice complicate its fulfillment, and one with a huge wild-card element, which I call (and apparently several people on cyberspace term) "sexpectation," or the expectation of a sexual experience with the man who is pursuing you. If the twenties and thirties have become a time for self-discovery and the building of an identity, then it's undeniable that some of the casualties of this trend are young women who are modern, Catholic, and professional — those who are capable, educated, marriage-minded women, who settle for casual sex and mediocre relationships, or who find the period of their single life extending years longer than they had anticipated.

The sense that there are no rules in dating anymore is not my unique observation. Goodness knows it's been going on for a few decades. However, it is my experience. If I had a dollar for every time I was confused about whether or not I was on a date when I was out with a man, I would have enough money to take them all out to dinner (which is subsequently another question that has emerged). Confusion about what constitutes a date, what is an appropriate way to invite someone to do something, who should pay for the event, and how to be clear about intentions or levels of interest are all up for grabs these days. And, as so aptly described in the movie *He's Just Not That into You*, there are entirely too many methods of communication, making the most basic types of human interaction so very inhumane:

> I had this guy leave me a voice mail at work so I called him at home and then he e-mailed me to my Blackberry and so I texted to his cell and then he e-mailed me to my home ac-

count and the whole thing just got out of control. And I miss the days when you had one phone number and one answering machine and that one answering machine has one cassette tape and that one cassette tape either had a message from a guy or it didn't. And now you just have to go around checking all these different portals just to get rejected by seven different technologies. It's exhausting.

The plethora of technologies is just one example of how this generation of self-identifiers has unending choices at our fingertips. Most of the people in my peer group had the resources to get a college education and the luxury of continuing the social side of college into our twenties. Without the self-sacrifice demanded of our grandparents at war or our parents in need of supporting themselves financially, we have been able to choose how to build our twenties and thirties: graduate school, international travel, and fulfilling personal goals have all been at our disposal, or at least on our radar.

With all of these opportunities and very few demands — especially as some of our parents continue to pay for our amenities — we have been able to extend our adolescence into what used to be considered adulthood. This extension has inevitably pushed off the questions of marriage and procreation, and when those questions are pushed further back into our personal timelines, dating loses its significance as a means to an end, though arguably also a good in itself. And without a direction, dating and relationships lose their rules, or at the very least, some general parameters.

In addition to having choices about what to do with our lives, our generation has a fairly large population of people to choose from when dating. I live in the Washington, D.C., area, which has a high concentration of smart, attractive people. I have heard young men and women here say that they hesitate to date one person because it's likely someone better will come along. However, even if one lives in a remote town, he or she can post on any number of dating websites and scour large directories of prospects. With so many options available, it is hard to fight the temptation to shop around until you find exactly what you're looking for. This quest for perfection, and the attitude of waiting until one finds it, is pervasive.

Further, though I can only give it brief mention here, it is clear from talking to female friends that the problem of pornography affects their relationships and dating experiences. I won't easily forget one situation that gave me a glimpse, albeit very small, into how this was affecting my friends. My date was giving me a tour of his house, and in one of his bedrooms he had a calendar of naked women hanging by his desk. I quietly made a remark about it, and he responded, "What, do you have a problem with that? I know you're Catholic, but you're not a nun." Had he simply asked *why* or *if* it made me feel uncomfortable, I think we could have had an interesting conversation. Instead, I felt like I was at fault for raising it as an issue at all. It is hard enough for any woman to battle feelings of inadequacy and sensitivity about her beauty or attractiveness. When compared to unrealistically thin and attractive women who are making their way both subtly and aggressively into our men's lives, we will always feel we fall short.

Moreover, I have heard from male friends that it is hard to fight the temptation to sit back and do nothing proactive in the arena of dating. To explain: When all of these factors intersect — the options, the lack of urgency to marry, the desire for perfection — women start champing at the bit and grasping for attention. Though there is something to be said for a woman having confidence and assertiveness in front of a man she is interested in, when she takes on the traditional role of men in the areas of sex and dating, apparently men simply stop acting. Male friends of mine have said that because women pursue *them*, they can be content with the casual hookup or with nonchalantly responding to women who are seeking their attention. I can't tell you the number of smart, beautiful women I know who are simply not being asked out, even when they are actively putting themselves in social situations. Again, if I had a dollar for each one, I'd take those girls out for consolation martinis or at least a therapeutic shopping spree. This lack of pursuit can easily lead to feelings of inadequacy for any woman; but for the Catholic woman, they may very well raise avoidable angst about vocation, purpose, and femininity.

If the initial questions of how to navigate the dating world were confusing and unclear, the expectations about sexual encounters are, in general, overwhelmingly clear. The expectation that you will be sexually intimate in a relationship — or with anyone with whom you go out for whatever duration — is now a given. I've had men tell me that my mere presence at a bar on a weekend night indicated that I was looking to hook up, and so I had no reason to be upset when they assumed I'd be sleeping with them that night. My mistake: I simply wanted a gin and tonic and some conversation with my girlfriends.

It is not uncommon to hear how this attitude of expected sexual intimacy has made its ways into a younger generation. A sixteen-year-old student I met at a conference told me about her friend's weekend experience and shared the following: "Yeah, I was so happy for her. It was her first hookup." "Her first kiss?" I asked. "No," she qualified, "her first hookup. You know, no strings attached and totally casual." If casual sexual encounters first became common on college campuses, they are now prevalent in middle school and high school. And since this young woman's experience mirrors that of my peers who are in their twenties or thirties and describing weekend hookups, it is becoming increasingly more difficult to propose to them a way of life that includes chastity, as their future relationship and dating prospects don't seem any more promising than their present experiences.

The assumption that a single woman, no matter her age, is having sex is pervasive. Young women talk about the pressure to "get sex over with before you go to college." Though I am not totally sure about the source of this pressure, I do believe it has to do in part with the ever-emerging nonchalance of teenage sex and pregnancy on television. Virginity seems to be something to lose as soon as possible, and its loss serves as a marker of maturity.[1] Gyms where I've been a member hang advertisements for birth control on the locker-room walls. At any ob-gyn visit, the idea of a virgin in her twenties or thirties is met with anything from curiosity to confusion to disdain. And, naturally, when certain men (though by no means all) find out on a date that you're not going to be sleeping with them, it's not unheard of that 1) you won't see their shadow from the cloud of dust they leave when they run away or 2) you are the girl that Billy Joel was describing in "Only the Good Die Young" and therefore ripe for conquest.

---

1 The best read on this is by Wendy Shalit, *Girls Gone Mild* (New York: Random House, 2007).

People simply don't know what to make of Catholic women who are sexual but are saving sex for marriage, who are accomplished working professionals, and who love fashion and design. Our way of life, instead of being a viable lifestyle choice, is often interpreted either as continued repression courtesy of our Church's "antiquated" moral teaching, or misconstrued as passing judgment on our peers who are sexually active or who see the world differently. It often feels like a lose-lose situation. However, I am increasingly hopeful that the culture will take us seriously as we become more vocal in the public square. Further, intentional, informed conversations about sex and dating — conversations in which we present the Catholic view clearly and convincingly — can do much to win hearts and minds. These interactions with individuals in the workplace, in our local bars, or at parties can have a great and lasting impact.

So What's the Catholic Girl to Do?

As the time of singlehood in a woman's life grows longer, she will inevitably face a variety of questions: What do I make of my single status? Do I date men who do not have my same moral frame of reference? Can I be taken seriously in my career if other professionals know that I am a practicing Catholic? Do I have a vocation "as is" in the Church? The answers to these questions will inevitably vary from person to person, and I will leave them to spiritual directors, theologians, and persons in the culture more equipped to address them than I.

To be sure, my relationship with Christ in and through the Catholic Church is the source of my identity. The great resources of the Church's spiritual writers, the ability to frequent the sacraments, the guidelines of her moral teaching, and the prayers and devotions I have in her treasury have grounded me in a way that nothing else has. As a young professional in the nation's capital, I am also fortunate to know many other young women who are well-educated, well-dressed, Catholic professionals trying to navigate the ever-growing tension between the religious and the secular worlds. But here's another problem: Though there are plenty of young, Catholic women like me, there seems to be a real lack of attention to the needs, questions, and desires of single Catholics in the Church.

Young-adult groups and Theology on Tap gatherings often feel like forced mating rituals. When giving homilies about vocations in the Church, priests always seem to add "the single life" under their breath, as if it's a default vocation or some unclear state of life. For those of us who find ourselves single, we can't help but exchange glances in the pew saying, "Do you feel like the leper Jesus was talking to or what?" It is not uncommon to go upward of a year or two between hearing a petitionary prayer for single people during Mass. Though the Church is exploding with blogs and on-line resources for laypeople, Catholic blogs for women seem to focus on natural family planning, fertility, and attachment parenting. To be honest, cervical mucus and debates on how long to breast-feed are not at the forefront of the working, single, Catholic woman's mind. And though it may seem trivial to be worrying about what clothes are work appropriate; whether or not five texts from a guy over the course of a week is an indication of his interest; or how to budget for car insurance, rental insurance, and a pair of knockoff designer flats — these questions reflect real trials in important virtues: modesty, economy, prudence.

The matter of the needs and contributions of single people in the Catholic Church is a pastoral problem requiring immediate attention, as the single population of those in their twenties, thirties, and forties continues to grow both in the country itself and in the Church. If the Church fails to pay regular, practical attention to the single, Catholic woman's situation, where is she to turn? As noted earlier, plenty of other sources will offer her options that will encourage her to settle for less than what she knows she can have. By trying to understand her life, the Church can help her battle against a life of mediocrity and offer crucial support toward a life of sanctity.

Carrie, of *Sex and the City* fame, once said: "It's really hard to walk in a single woman's shoes — that's why you sometimes need really special shoes!" I call upon the Church and the culture to understand the experience of the single, Catholic woman. She has much to contribute. Ask her about her daily life, and she will inevitably enrich yours. Hers is an identity that can be mined for riches, an identity that you need to acknowledge and affirm. Step into her shoes and walk a mile. It's worth it.

Elise Italiano teaches at a college preparatory high school in the Washington, D.C., area. She has a master's degree in theology from Villanova University and a B.A. in humanities from Providence College.

Chapter 4

Finding Joy
The Mystery of
the Religious Life

Sister Mary Gabriel, S.V.

 A life of renunciation, seeming distance from the ups and downs of ordinary life, black lace-up shoes — if this is all one knows of religious life, it can seem a pretty dim prospect, even to Catholics. I admit there was a time in my life when I, too, might have concluded that this was the extent of a religious vocation, and I would have responded "no thanks" (had I thought about it at all). If the story ended there, the loss for me would have been unimaginable.

Catholic women have been living the religious life for centuries. Despite what some may think, it has never been part of an oppressive plan by the hierarchy to keep women in their place. While religious life is aimed at holiness and not at accomplishing anything in a worldly sense, this vocation has been a showcase for the creative talents and generous energy of women. From the development of the early American Catholic school system by Mother Elizabeth Ann Seton in the early 1800s to the orphanages and hospitals run by Mother Frances Cabrini to the more recent worldwide influence of

Mother Teresa and her missionary sisters who care for the poor, Catholic women religious have had an irreplaceable impact on culture and society. But it doesn't take a superstar to live this vocation to the hilt: the most hidden of religious have cared for the poor, forgotten, lonely, sick, and broken-hearted — all those with no one to defend them. Spiritual maternity has long been entrusted to consecrated women.

I learned this fact soon after entering the Sisters of Life thirteen years ago. The Sisters of Life are dedicated to the protection and enhancement of every human life. To that end we house and support pregnant women in need, host spiritual retreats, offer accompaniment toward healing to those who have suffered abortion, and direct the Respect Life offices for the Archdiocese of New York and the Diocese of Bridgeport. Spiritual maternity, however, extends far beyond the walls of our missions.

It doesn't matter whether it's the daily Massgoing grandmother who slips me a paper with the names of her grandchildren; the non-Catholic young woman filling gas next to me who, without hesitation, asks me with sadness about her friend who just died of cancer; or the heavy-metal-band member on a plane who shyly introduces himself to me with, "Well, I'm not much of a praying man, but..." I'm theirs. I'm theirs because I'm God's. And people of every stripe seem to know it intuitively.

One of the most frequently asked questions I receive, after "What community are you with?" and "Do you sleep in that?" (referring to our habit) is, "Why did you become a sister?"

There's only one reason any woman would enter and follow religious life: love. Not the idea of love, or the need to serve for the sake of love, but *really* love, a call of love from

Jesus and a response of love in return. This love delights and surprises; it captures the heart and fulfills the person called in a way no other manner of life could. Though there are many renunciations, ours is not a life of deprivation.

Some sisters knew they were called at a young age. Even for them — after years of tying towels around their heads like veils and secretly writing out possible religious names in the backs of notebooks — this vocation is anything but a calculated decision. For me, it was most certainly not calculated: I didn't connect the dots that I was being called until after college. Once I did, a peace and joy I couldn't fabricate followed. I've never looked back.

Making Space for Grace

Though I grew up going to Sunday Mass with my family, and I continued that practice into college, a personal relationship with God was not prominent in my life. In fact, I kept God at arm's length. Perhaps it was because my understanding of him was connected with limitations. Perhaps it was because I felt interiorly divided. Perhaps I thought I had to have it all figured out before I could sincerely come to him. Whatever it was, at some point midway through college I knew that something had to give. I wanted a deeper relationship with God, but I had no idea how to make that happen at the level of the heart. That was discouraging in itself. I thought I should know — after all, I went to Catholic school. I got A's in religion class. But I didn't know. What if what I had *was* all there was to the spiritual life?

Since I didn't know how to pray, there was only one way to find out — I went to the chapel and watched others pray.

My time there often ended with new to-do lists, inner commentary on who should or shouldn't be dating whom, and reviews of the dessert served that night, but my very desire became the prayer the Lord heard.

In the midst of this dissatisfaction, I crossed campus late on a warm spring night as I had countless times before, from the library to my dorm. This time, though, my walk was interrupted by an undeniable pull as I approached the chapel. It was as if the chapel came to me. When I opened the heavy door and walked into the glow of the red sanctuary lamp flickering in the darkness, the chapel was empty, but I knew I wasn't alone. The peace I felt was unmistakably the peace of Jesus.

I fell to my knees, with nothing to give but myself, however unimpressive that seemed to me. In those moments, all I had been taught about God as a child became real to me, and I knew this God loved me in a deeply personal way. It was the beginning of living fully.

This encounter was pivotal for me, but it didn't answer all my questions. I still separated my intellectual life from my budding personal faith. I didn't understand all the Church teachings, especially those that touched on hot-button issues, and I hadn't made much effort to do so.

I was, however, fascinated with women's role in society and the Church. When the United Nations Commission on the Status of Women convened in Beijing in 1995, I watched intently and with curiosity, reading every article, and from every possible angle. I was impressed by the progress women had made over the last century; I relished the emerging of women into greater prominence and respect in society. It seemed the true potential of women was beginning to be revealed to the world, and I loved it — so much so that I seriously considered pursuing a graduate degree in women's studies. But I didn't connect this interest with my faith.

This lack on my part became like a storm cloud on the horizon, a brewing conflict in my interior. At some point, I would need to address it, and, as with most things in my life, I didn't want to wait. If I was going to be Catholic for the rest of my life, I wanted to be able to sincerely say yes to everything the Church teaches and to know why I was saying yes to it. If I couldn't say yes, I didn't want to live as if I were — I desired integration and authenticity. When I mentioned this to friends, I found I wasn't alone. We decided to each take a topic, research, and then share both the whys of that Church teaching as well as opposing views.

The topic I received was birth control. I read everything I could get my hands on. While the Church's position was appealing in that it harmonized with everything else the Church thought, I understood the "outraged" response. It seemed irrational that a woman should be caught between a career (or the development of her spousal relationship, or any personal plans) and the overwhelming prospect of raising numerous children, when all could be managed peacefully with a little help from contraception. My head tried to grasp Church teaching — my heart faltered.

In the midst of my intentional grappling, I was again, surprisingly, drawn to the chapel. My two worlds were brought together. I found myself before the God who loved me without knowing whether I believed what this Church said was true. I simply told him that, and waited for him to answer.

I went into that chapel in one state of mind and heart, and left completely different. It was the first time I can remember receiving the Spirit's gift of understanding. In the course of my sitting before the Lord, sharing with him my real questions and resistance, the teaching unfolded and made sense to me. It all clicked. It didn't just click in an intellectual way, but I perceived a real tenderness in it. I saw that the teaching was *for* women; it was *for* me.

That I didn't have to struggle with unresolved issues disconnected from the Lord brought a relief to my soul that I didn't know I needed until I had it. He wanted me to bring my misgivings and misunderstandings to him. My lack of certainty didn't keep him from me in the least.

My confidence in the Lord jumped. I could say, and do say, to anyone wrestling with a difficult situation or decision — just park in front of the Blessed Sacrament and bring it honestly to Jesus. He'll hear you, love you, and answer you. Maybe not right away, maybe not in the way you expect, but he will answer.

Love Revolution

It was good that I learned this, because I was still every bit the unpredictable college student, and I needed to park myself before the Blessed Sacrament many times over. Still, I wouldn't have dreamt of the convent. No one talked about the possibility of religious life, and it never crossed my mind. I wanted to get married — and presumed I would — and raise a family, preferably of rambunctious boys. I presumed graduate school, followed by a life in academia or public policy and advocacy work. But like my total immersion in the delights of collegiate life, all these plans were on the surface. I knew somewhere underneath it all that my trajectory was off. I had a strange intuition that I wouldn't see the other side of my plans. I had no idea why that was, but I told my mother, to her horror, that I was convinced it was because I would die young.

Six months after graduating, I was living the dream in New York City. I spent my days working on the Upper East Side, my evenings reconnecting with old friends in Manhattan. It soon became evident that others were comfortable with the way their lives were unfolding. I, on the other hand, was restless inside. I wanted to give more, love more, live for more. I began spending my Saturdays in the South Bronx with the Franciscans, a religious order, helping the poor. There I found a joy and freedom missing from the other parts of my life, however interesting and entertaining they were. It was cause for pause.

I began praying more. And then a lot more. I skipped out on parties to go to Holy Hours. I would find random churches in New York and join the old ladies praying the Rosary after Mass. And I truly didn't feel like I was missing out on anything. I had to admit that something unusual was happening. This was not normal. My friends were definitely not doing this. I didn't even have words to name it, but the possibility of religious life hovered over my heart. I wondered, more than a bit concerned — does this actually still happen to people, people like me?

I wasn't immune to the fact that religious life meant poignant sacrifices. I thought of living without marriage and a family of my own and wondered: Could I live happily? Would I be lonely? The not-so-poignant sacrifices became present to me, too. Every so often, I had an aching dread in the pit of my stomach when I thought about the practicalities of convent life. I had to guess it was a far cry from what I was used to.

When I had free time, this possibility returned, ever stronger. One evening as I walked down Lexington Avenue during rush hour, people frantically pushing by on their way from work, I finally wanted an answer more than I wanted control over my own life. I entered the next church I passed and knelt before the Blessed Sacrament, ready to yield to whatever he wanted of me. Jesus answered as if he had been waiting at the gates. As I had experienced in college, there was no doubt in whose presence I was. But this time in prayer, I felt my heart align with another's, with his, and connect. It was a love unlike any other I had experienced before, and I knew what it meant. I wasn't thinking or speaking, but there was only one response — yes, from the depths of my soul. I didn't care if it meant scrubbing floors with toothbrushes or a lifetime of black lace-up shoes or living with strange people who would wonder how someone like me ended up with them. It was worth it. I left that time of prayer more alive than I had ever been.

If I thought I had been emotional before that, I hadn't seen anything yet. Life became high definition and in surround sound. Everything — I mean everything — was beautiful to me. When I wasn't grinning ear to ear, I was weeping for beauty. My heart leapt out, even to strangers. I was amazed at their goodness; I ached for their every suffering and sin. But it didn't stop at that. Every movie I watched moved me to the depths. It was embarrassing. The poor man sitting next to me on a plane back from California had to be confused while I watched *The Prince of Egypt*. Granted, it was about the Exodus, but it was a cartoon, for crying out loud, and there I was, a slobbering mess. No doubt about it, I was in love, and with God.

Telling people the news was nerve-racking on one hand and a fascinating study on the other. One of my friends dropped the phone in shock. A coworker thought it was another outrageous joke I was playing — it took him a week of convincing and a trip to the convent before he would believe it. My next-door neighbor welled up with tears, and with great gentleness urged in protest, "But you're so good with children!" I will never forget my father, days after I informed him of my decision, leaning back against the kitchen counter with a pensive look on his face, looking at me deeply. "What is it, Dad?" I asked. "What about everything you wanted to do…" was all he could get out.

His answer surprised me, because his concern hadn't crossed my happy heart. But my father knew me. He knew all I had wanted from life, and this was something altogether different. Love has a way of turning our plans on their heads, and it teaches us something wonderful in the process.

Too often the value of a person is judged — either by herself or others — by wealth, relationships, power, or the lack thereof. One of the gifts of the religious life is to reveal to the world that God measures all of us — religious, single, or married — not according to material standards, but according to who we are in him. When a woman vows poverty, chastity, and obedience, what she has left is simply her person — not what she can do, not what she has in terms of money, not her talents or education, not any defining clan of people. The religious life has always and will always witness to the startling value of one human soul — every human soul — in the sight of God.

Setting Captives Free

Perhaps partly because we've renounced the material gains and professional and social status so emphasized in our culture, the religious vocation offers an entry for others into a larger reality. Regardless of whether I am a "success" in the eyes of the world, I can be received as I am, good and lovable. When this, in fact, happens, so do miracles. Time and again I've seen in those I serve a transformation of heart that echoes my own experience: the revolution of coming to know that God is real and actually loves me; the peace of knowing he forgives me and isn't afraid of my wounds; the hope sparked in recognizing that he intends greatness for me and has written it on my heart.

When a woman comes to us, whether she's in a crisis pregnancy, is confounded by her abortion experience, or is just generally lost or hurting, what she often needs first is to be received without judgment, to be listened to and loved for who she is, not for what she has or hasn't done. It is astounding to realize the extent of the hidden burdens carried by the women we live with, work with, pray with, see every day — and presume all is well. There are secret sufferings of long-ago sin, the anguish of infertility, betrayals of spouses, children lost to addictions. What no one else may know — not even the closest of friends — can be and is shared in confidence with a sister. Religious are essentially neither social workers nor sounding boards, though they may be both at any moment, without any warning.

I was stunned as a novice when, as I was out for a bicycle ride with a professed sister, she flew off her bike and landed — sprawled out — on what had been a beautifully manicured bush on someone's front lawn. My second thought, after noting she wasn't hurt, was to worry about the owner's response to the beautiful bush. A woman came running out of the house, but the interaction was quite different than what I had feared. She bent over the sister, saying through tears, "You are an angel sent to me by God! He heard me!" It turns out that this woman, long away from the faith, was in the middle of a bitter and painful divorce and at the end of her rope. Right before this sister went hurtling through the air into her bushes, this woman had prayed her first sincere prayer in years: "God, I can't do this without you. Please send me a sign that you still care about me."

Sometimes we come to people; other times they come to us. Last year I took the novices out for a well-deserved picnic lunch at the beach. We had just plopped ourselves down on the sand in a long semicircle and pulled out our brown bags when two young women walked by and greeted us with an enthusiastic, "Oh my gosh, who are you?" A return greeting prompted the two, both seniors in high school, to take up their posts at either end of the semicircle, each claiming a group of sisters for themselves. One was a nominal Catholic, the other a Seventh-day Adventist. They had no idea we would be at the beach that day, but their questions were ready at hand. As they spoke with all the drama and passion of seventeen year olds, I was struck by their beauty, honesty, and trust. I was sitting with one who shared, at first with embarrassment and then with greater ease, her current struggle: her Church friends were good influences, but her school friends were into binge drinking. She kept following, and she kept falling. She didn't like her behavior with them, but she didn't want to lose their friendship. She asked us what she should do. All we did was ask her the right questions, and she quickly saw that she already had the answer — she knew what she had to do.

When they left us, the two of them almost skipped down the beach. The wisdom of the world that says, "Do what you want in the moment," left this young woman, as it leaves all of us, confused and in situations of regret. When she perceived there was space for her — regrets and all — in another's heart, it was a lot easier to access the good that never changes and to allow herself to guide her actions by it.

None of us are that far off from this seventeen-year-old. There's a lot of noise in our busy world. It's easy to distrust our hearts, to get discouraged. It's hard to hear the whisper of truth deep within. All of us need to be received by others, to have our fundamental goodness affirmed. Then we can love in a way that sets others free. The more I know myself to be loved, the easier it is to give others that same gift.

When one of our guests, let's call her Tiffany, came to live with us, she made it clear, in her quiet and sweet way, that while she was choosing to have her child, she could never tell another woman what to do with a pregnancy. As the months rolled on, we simply loved Tiffany — and she was very easy to love.

One evening, she came home from a doctor's appointment unusually excited to tell the sisters about her day. She had been at a New York hospital that delivers babies on one floor and has an abortion clinic on another. She got on the elevator and was joined by another woman. When Tiffany said hello, this woman burst into tears and said, "I'm pregnant." Tiffany's response? "Congratulations! I'm pregnant, too." The woman shook her head and said she just couldn't have this baby. Right then, Tiffany felt her own baby moving in her womb, and she placed the woman's hand on her own belly just in time for a power kick. The woman said, "Wow!" "Yeah, my baby's going to be a linebacker," Tiffany laughed. "He's going to be strong, and he's going to be blessed." "Why will he be blessed?" the woman asked. "Because he's here," Tiffany responded. "Whether you cry, or you laugh, if you're here, you're blessed. You're put here for a reason."

The woman said, "I'm going to have an abortion." Without missing a beat, Tiffany said, "No you're not. You are going to have a girl. I know that already because I wanted to have a girl, but I'm having a boy, but that's OK — you have your girl and dress her up in pink. Put ponytails in her hair and call her Tiffany, and by the way, my middle name is Rose. And if she asks you how she got her name, tell her you met a fabulous lady on the elevator one day who was pregnant, and she told you that you were going to have a beautiful little girl."

They got out of the elevator together, and Tiffany walked with the woman to make an appointment with her own obstetrician.

The two didn't stay in contact, but two years later Tiffany regaled us with the conclusion of the story. She had returned to that same hospital for a routine checkup when, out of the blue, a woman pushing a stroller ran up to her and hugged her. She had twins — two girls. Their names: Tiffany and Rose, and both were dressed up in pink. She said, "I love you. You don't understand, Tiffany: I love you. I love you. I love you. I'll never forget your name, your face, your smile. I would do anything for you. I love you." To which Tiffany responded, "I love you, too. I understand. I have experienced it."

Knowing one's own goodness and dignity — that I am known and loved by God — has a way of unleashing the gift of self, the power to love others, in a way that sets them free and heals us at the same time. Ultimately, this is what so many women, myself included, have searched for. This is the unrelenting whisper in the heart, the truth that refuses to go away. The more we trust this truth and live it out, letting God show us that, in fact, his power *is* made perfect in weakness, the more easily we — individually and collectively — will step into the world saying with confidence and joy, "Here we are."

Sister Mary Gabriel, S.V., is a member of the Sisters of Life, a New York-based community of consecrated women religious dedicated to protecting and enhancing the sacredness of human life. Originally from Long Island, New York, she has been a member of the Sisters of Life since 1999 and currently serves as novice director for the community.

Chapter 5

Something Old and Something Really New
Women as Professionals and Breadwinners, but Pilgrims Just the Same

Mary Devlin Capizzi, J.D.

 I have always worked. My first job was a newspaper route that I inherited from my two older brothers. When the route was mine, I would ride my bike after school more than a mile each way to pick up the papers and deliver them to the customers on my street. It didn't take long for the paper route to turn a profit. Unlike my brothers, who never collected from all their customers, I made sure I covered expenses and made a profit. I came to recognize that I enjoyed the independence of working and the deep satisfaction that comes from observing the fruitfulness of one's own hard work. I also learned some things about myself. Undertaking a job with the right spirit could be deeply, personally satisfying. I could find a way through my work to serve and connect more deeply with others. And I had particular gifts that were magnified through my working.

Beyond tossing a paper on a step, I enjoyed getting to know my customers and helping them. In some cases the help was simply responding to a particular request, such as ringing the doorbell when I brought the paper, or making sure I started my delivery route with their house. My budding sense of the importance of courtesy and the satisfaction of deepening bonds of connection profited my soul — and in all honesty my pocket too. Doing my best revealed my character to others and my passion for work: tips grew; customers multiplied; and one job led to another — babysitting, housesitting, petsitting.

Midway through high school, I gave up the newspaper route but took up other work which continued through college and law school. All through this time, my parents sent a steady message to all their children about the virtue of hard work. They were neither impressed with job status nor inclined to encourage any of us to pursue a line of work because it could earn a lot of money or prestige. They took our musings about potential work seriously and never discouraged the articulated possibilities (for example, in my case, fashion industry buyer, personal shopper, international business person, author, translator, boss) because they believed our chosen work, whatever that would be, could serve as an instrument to living a well-examined and virtuous life.

The Catholic faith was an integral part of our family life. My parents read Church documents and always seemed connected to wider conversations on theology, ethics, and philosophy. They were persuaded by the truth and reasonableness of Catholic teachings. They did their best, at the same time, to cultivate the human and spiritual gifts of their mostly rambunctious but occasionally charming children. At times, having thoughtful, observant Catholic parents seemed like a real burden. During high school, I often wished quietly (and sometimes out loud) that I was born into a family that thought less about the meaning of life and more about taking me to the mall.

I perceived early on that my father put no limits on what his daughters could do. This was a crucial foundation for my later life as both lawyer and parent. He was tender when it came to parenting us — he was patient, affirmed us regularly, and constantly marveled out loud at the individuals we were becoming. He had trained in philosophy and taught college for a time, but he made a career as a commercial artist. He impressed upon me several things: that education was a serious privilege, to be undertaken first and foremost for gaining wisdom; and that we were to grow not only in academic wisdom, but always, too, in our Catholic faith.

My mother, a nurse, was the oldest child in an Irish immigrant family and was de facto a leader in her family. Her parents had little formal education and had relied upon their oldest child to help them navigate many aspects of their life in the United States. In my home life, my mother dealt much more with the practicalities of child-rearing than my father, and she was strong, consistent, and hardworking. My father respected her voice as an equal. It was a model I did and do admire.

While my immigrant grandmother, my mother, and I had dramatically different educational, social, and professional opportunities, our work ethic and Catholic faith have been constant across three generations. Braided together, these have enabled our accomplishments, whether as a housewife rearing three children (my grandmother), or as a mother devoted to rearing six children at home and at times working as a nurse (my mother), or as a partner in a large corporate law firm who also holds leadership roles in the community, while sharing with my husband the joys and demands of rearing six children (me). When viewed through the lens of our shared faith, the real differences between three generations of women seem less dramatic. Each of us has recognized faith as our touchstone, received as a gift and passed on. Just as for my grandmother and mother, my faith has never held me back nor limited me, but rather guided and strengthened me.

Growing a Family and a Career

I left college with a B.A. in Spanish literature and an M.B.A. in international management. My first job was as a legal assistant to a team of bankers and lawyers restructuring the debt of Latin American countries. This stretched and steered me, highlighting for me the importance of organizational dynamics in the workplace. While colleagues were often well-educated and talented, that alone was not enough. I saw how essential it was that people worked well together. I also observed that notwithstanding a high degree of education and training, many were unhappy in their jobs. I perceived that for some there was no meaningful connection to or satisfaction with their work, and I promised myself that I would not let this happen to me. Working side by side with well-educated and often privileged colleagues, I gained confidence in my gifts as a talented worker.

After two years of this, I decided to study law. I met my husband during law school. I wasn't looking to meet a husband. In fact, I was pretty sure that I could be content never marrying. Every young man interested in dating me had the — I assume unintended — effect of annoying me. My husband was a graduate student studying theological ethics. He was raised Catholic, and when we met he was slowly making his way back to the Church after leaving it behind in high school. He was never threatened by my ambition or professional interests, and we early recognized that our work paths (his as an academic and mine as a lawyer) would be very different. Our relationship flourished because he allowed me to be myself. I attribute much of that to his own upbringing — he is comfortable in his own skin and confident of his own educational and professional path (and was raised by an affirming, sensitive, and intelligent Jewish mother). We married one year after I completed law school, when he was finishing his doctorate in theology at Notre Dame and I was a law firm associate in Chicago.

The first of our six children was born a year after I joined the firm. My salary became — and has remained — the primary source of our family's income. While income disparity between a husband and a wife can be a source of dramatic tension, we have managed it fairly well. That is not to say I have navigated it gracefully and patiently at all times. There have been times when the stress of full-time legal work, demanding international travel, and being the primary breadwinner, as well as the reality that I have had less time with my children, has made me resentful. I have daydreamed about a reality that is not mine — enjoying carefree summers with my children on Lake Winnipesaukee in New Hampshire, subsidized by my husband's big paycheck (or hearty trust fund — either would work). I have pondered out loud the merits of leaving the Washington, D.C., area and moving to a rural

Virginian farm where I could learn to cook and garden and home-school. (This dream always provokes vigorous laughter from those who know me well, including my children. I can neither cook nor garden and am a poor teacher).

I recall several times when, with great insensitivity, I highlighted for my husband the injustice that his sharp mind and many years of study are not adequately compensated, and that his salary made it impossible for me to have the option of staying home. But despite those passing moments of irritation and sore pride, I am confident that God played a role in bringing us together, with our particular gifts and vocations, and I have been able to embrace my work as my calling, a terrain that challenges and rewards me intellectually, emotionally, spiritually, and economically. I recognize that my job has enabled us to support our family.

I also have the opportunity to integrate my faith into my daily life in the office, and this has enabled me to see how grace flourishes in unlikely places. While from the outside a law firm can seem like a sterile and soulless place, my work environment has been interesting, affirming, and collaborative. My colleagues have consistently been supportive of my growing family. Obviously, this is not every woman's experience, let alone every lawyer's. My firm supported me during maternity leaves. Senior colleagues encouraged the strength of a functional and productive team, which included me, a mother of a growing family. In turn, I learned to delegate, to remain flexible enough to do the work required when it was required (even during my maternity leaves), and to determine which areas of law practice are better suited than others for getting home to dinner.

Balance and Teamwork

At the same time, I would never describe my experience as spiritually or emotionally "smooth." With almost every pregnancy I initially felt torn. I struggled to integrate two parts of myself that were seemingly at odds. There was the personal side, whose heart knew that welcoming a child was a natural and beautiful consequence of a loving marriage and would no doubt enrich our family in the long term. There was also the driven, ambitious, professional side that immediately became vulnerable and anxious. Notwithstanding that my husband has handled many of the demands of a busy family — picking up the children from school most days, helping with homework, doing almost all the cooking — and that we have had wonderful baby sitters and housecleaners for additional help … when staring at a positive pregnancy test, the questions and doubts would still race through my mind: What other associate has had a baby? Can I make it to month seven without anyone knowing? How can I do this again?

There were times I felt very weak and unsure, and even a little embarrassed. Yet as anyone who has suffered knows, it is when we are weak and vulnerable that we are most open to letting our faith live. I needed the lifeline of faith, and I grabbed it — especially in those first months of each pregnancy. My prayers were heard. In each case, I would undergo a dramatic transformation. Instead of being defensive about a new baby, I became able to appreciate the gift of fertility, something not extended to all. Importantly, over time, I gained a perspective that nine months pass pretty quickly and that the years with our children are fleeting. This is a perspective that parents regularly gain, and those fearful of parenting should by all means be exposed to it. Finally, often, my work colleagues were easier on me than I was on myself, although I am keenly aware that this is not every woman's experience.

Living at a time of limitless educational and professional pathways for women is in many ways remarkable. Today I have at my disposal a broad toolkit that includes my education and my now lengthy work experience. The opportunities afforded to me would have been unimaginable to my grandmother who arrived in New York City in 1926 from Ireland with little education and spent a lifetime dedicated to homemaking. She was still baking Irish soda bread in 2010, the year she died at age 100. But the opportunities available to women today are not at odds with Catholic teachings or our ability to model our lives after the saints; everything depends upon our response and whether, ultimately, we use these opportunities for service — service to God, to the families given to us, and to all those we encounter through work.

The difficult aspects of my work as a business lawyer are not unique. Any woman, regardless of her state in life, can relate to the challenges I face as a wife and working mother. We don't have enough time to do all we need to do for ourselves, our families, or our work. We worry, feel underappreciated or even disrespected, and yearn to have our efforts acknowledged. At the same time, Catholics are exhorted to remember that our challenges are opportunities to refine ourselves, to struggle to be more faithful. They remind us, relentlessly, of how dependent we are on God's continual generosity and grace.

My upbringing prepared me well for the work life. I never had a sense that women were relegated to specific spheres or that there were limitations on what I could do because I was female. Rather, my parents encouraged all of us children, regardless of gender, to use our gifts and talents in whatever way God called us. My reality is this: I make more money than my husband, and our large family relies on my income. But tempering the disparity in our incomes is our recognition that the real work of our lives belongs to us both fully and jointly. There is a lot of talk in the popular (and even scholarly) press about women's need to insist that husbands take on at least 50 percent of the domestic work. We avoided that kind of "accounting," and it's been one of the healthiest decisions we ever made. My husband and I understand and recognize that each of us brings unique gifts and energy to our marriage, and each of us does what we're good at. (Interestingly, there is also a lot of current literature indicating that an "accounting" mentality is poison to a marriage, while a "gift" mentality sustains it.) There was a certain amount of family disapproval of our arrangement. In the early years of our marriage, my mother-in-law would sometimes say that she thought her son was doing too much. Some years ago she came to me with beautiful humility and apologized; she acknowledged all we both did and said she had come to love how our family hummed along in its unique way.

While my work has provided financially for our family, my husband's temperament, intellect, patience, and academic scheduling flexibility have been key. He brings his undivided presence to our marriage and family. While I have a lot of energy, I am also distracted by all that remains to be done — the pending projects, unfinished emails, the next business opportunity, unwritten thank-you notes, undone laundry, the children's sports schedule. In my frenzied quest to get everything done, I often overlook the need just to be. This is where my husband helps, pulling me back from the distractions in which I often get stuck. He firmly but lovingly reminds me that nothing I have on my to-do list is, for example, more important than eating together whenever possible, listening (really listening) to my teenage daughters, helping my six-year-old learn to ride a bicycle, or reading to our youngest children before they go to sleep. Being present is priceless, and it is a gift my husband has given to me and our children. It is unquestionably worth much more than any paycheck I have earned. I am clear on this, even as it contradicts the world's wisdom. I think it is part of the gift of faith I have been given by God and by my parents and husband.

It would be hard — likely impossible in fact — to imagine that I would have attained my professional success or domestic happiness without it being deeply rooted in the stability of my faith. Faith, not my work, is the root that defines my life, and my work reflects and reveals my faith. This has been an evolution — a work in progress.

Ironically, with more opportunities, women are more inclined to be hard on themselves. We feel pressured to accomplish a checklist of goals that validate "success." We see signs of this everywhere, ranging from the magnets on the back of Chevy Suburbans that advertise certain high schools and colleges, "travel" sports teams, and coveted vacation spots, to the restlessness many women experience regardless of whether they work full time, part time, or always at home. Here, again, our faith helps us. While our work can be integrated with our faith, our faith is clear that our work could never completely define or validate us.

I carry prayer with me as I work. I need it every day. I call on particular saints to give me guidance. (St. Joseph the

Worker is a favorite — I have his prayer card on my desk.) I try, with different levels of success, to love my clients and colleagues as individuals worthy of my best respect, efforts, and time. My hard work, whether interesting or dull, is a concrete way to express my love, if done with a spirit of service. In parallel, at home, a shared faith has been essential in understanding and supporting each other in our respective work.

To my mind, there is no controversy in the diversity in which a woman or a man can live out one's vocation in the world. Far from it. Each of us, regardless of our unique experience and circumstances, is called by our faith to love and serve God. I have been stung by some women judging me by my situation — as if my work has made me a less faithful Catholic, a worse wife, or a neglectful mother. On several occasions I have been told that I am working only to satisfy myself and that I "really don't have to work." I have also experienced working women who are quick to judge mothers who stay at home to rear children or, God forbid, home-school. I recall an exchange in which someone started mocking home-schooling; it was delightful to me to move the conversation away from caricatures as I reported that a most admired and beloved sister (an Ivy League college graduate, All-American and All-Ivy athlete, and mother) home-schooled all of her children! We all miss something by categorizing each other without respecting that women can and do live vastly different yet good lives. There is no a priori way every woman must live her faith, and Catholic teaching does not consider work outside the home a mere concession to financial realities or the result of a false vocation.

Women find themselves in many different situations. A woman who thought she would be married by thirty remains single for her entire life. A stay-at-home mother returns to full-time work, and her husband starts running the household after his job is eliminated and no viable work options are available to him. An elderly mother of a grown family finds herself caring both for a husband with Alzheimer's and a son who has returned from war severely wounded, while her middle-aged daughter returns to the family home after an unfaithful husband squanders shared financial resources and abandons her. A mother of young children feels a strong tug to finish her long-neglected dissertation and adds her much-needed voice to Catholic social concerns. A clinical psychologist with an academic appointment at a prestigious university joins a new Catholic order of religious sisters. A mother of eight adult children assumes the role of mother to her grandson, an infant boy, after her own son's young immigrant wife dies a week after childbirth; she becomes the person to whom her grandson attributes his deep Catholic formation. A single mother converts to Catholicism and spends a lifetime serving the poor and homeless and advocating nonviolence. These are all real Catholic women. Life is unpredictable and at times gritty. Our lives don't fit neatly in pre-designed boxes — nor should we expect them to.

Guided by Faith

Notwithstanding our diverse paths or unique circumstances as Christian women we always have the possibility of giving our lives over to God and trusting him to lead us where he wills. The voices of doubt, the insecurities, the harsh aspects of a competitive world, and even the wounds we carry can be pacified and put into proper context by the reality of a

God who knows us (in all our confusion and complexity) and desires our happiness. He has given us, too, remarkable role models among female Catholic saints, none of whom had a smooth, untroubled life, but all of whom came to trust wholly in a loving and merciful God regardless of their circumstances.

Two of my favorites include Teresa of Avila and Thérèse of Lisieux. St. Teresa is an obvious role model for a woman pursuing worldly impact. She was a figure of international consequence in sixteenth-century Spain! She reformed the Carmelite order and established thirty-two new convents, was strategic, intelligent, a correspondent of King Philip II, industrious, courageous, and all the while very, very funny. Her faith was not incompatible with her work; in fact, it was the most notable gift she brought to her work.

St. Thérèse, at first glance, is not an obvious role model for today's woman. She entered a cloistered convent at fifteen and never left it — she died of tuberculosis at twenty-four years old. Some of the sisters in her order considered her life so ordinary that they wondered how anyone would be able to write her obituary. Nevertheless, her "little" life, tucked away in a cloister, has left an unmistakable legacy: she relied on God explicitly for every step of her journey toward learning to love and learning to believe. Regardless of where we find ourselves as women, this is a journey we must make as well. Thérèse's "little way" has provided the template for countless women, no matter their vocation in this world. Thérèse promised that she would spend her heaven doing good on earth; I explicitly rely on her for advice and guidance in many matters at work, at home, and elsewhere. I have also encouraged my school-age daughters to befriend Thérèse and to rely on her guidance and example of love. When one of my daughters was suffering social pressures during the fourth grade, we found one of those great pictures of young Thérèse and put it in the transparent sleeve of her binder. She stayed there as the face of the plastic pink binder all during that school year, helping my daughter navigate these challenges with grace and self-confidence.

I am grateful for the Church and her wisdom. I see God's mercy and generosity in many aspects of my life: in my grandparents who passed on the gift of their faith; in my parents who nourished the gift of faith and gave me freedom to cultivate my gifts without limits; in my husband who has loved me unconditionally and without any insecurity about my professional path or earning power; in my six children who have pulled me away from seeking external approval and held me accountable (often with good humor) to be present to them; in my siblings and extended family members; in my work colleagues and clients; and in my enduring friendships. I am grateful that society today allows benefits and opportunities to women that were unheard of in prior generations. These opportunities, when integrated with our faith, allow women to recognize and cultivate their gifts and witness the faithfulness and mercy of our loving God.

> Let nothing disturb you; Let nothing frighten you. All things are passing. God never changes. Patience obtains all things. Nothing is wanting to him who possesses God. God alone suffices. — St. Teresa of Avila

Mary Devlin Capizzi is a lawyer in Washington, D.C., and a member of her firm's government relations and regulatory affairs group. Her legal practice includes counseling on regulatory, legislative, and policy issues and serving as legal counsel and secretariat for industry consortia in the life sciences industry. She lives in Maryland with her husband and their five daughters and one son.

Chapter 6

The Sexual Abuse Scandal
The Great Wound of Our Era and Its Challenge

Rebecca Vitz Cherico, Ph.D.

Probing the Wound

Why is my pain unceasing, my wound incurable, refusing to be healed? — Jeremiah 15:18

I recently heard a talk given by a psychologist. The subject was marriage, but I could see the analogy to the sex-abuse scandal in the Church. In discussing the difficulty of loving one's spouse, he remarked that people will do a lot to avoid pain, including getting angry at a loved one because heated anger can be an adaptation for avoiding painful situations. As applied to the sex-abuse scandal in the Church, anyone can see that there is a great deal of anger out there — righteous anger often, but also perhaps anger as a means to avoid suffering. Given, however, that Christianity preaches Christ crucified as well as Christ resurrected, it seems that we must confront the pain of this crisis before we can experience anything like a resurrection.

Yet there has been so much dishonesty and misinformation surrounding the scandal, so much broken trust, that many Catholics simply don't know whom to believe anymore, so the painful wound festers instead of being given the chance to heal. Still, having thought about this issue a great deal and followed its unfolding in one of the "hotbed" dioceses — Philadelphia — if there is anything that I have learned, it is that no evil is so great that Christ cannot overcome it.

The sexual abuse scandal is less of a "women's concern" than many other challenges facing the Church today. The scandal was perpetrated mostly by male priests and religious on younger males; those accused of mishandling it are, likewise, male hierarchy. And yet, as we try to grapple with the challenge of the scandal, I believe that feminine wisdom can shed light on the situation and the possibilities for justice and healing. Women have been suffering at the foot of the cross since the very earliest days of the Church, when most of Jesus' followers had deserted him. We have a history of bearing with Jesus through moments of scandal. Now is a time of scandal if ever there was. We must again demonstrate our willingness to stay with Christ, with the Church, while simultaneously insisting that rendering the fullest possible justice for victims renders the Church what Jesus intended.

A native New Yorker, I moved to the Philadelphia archdiocese in 2002. At first, in light of the terrible priest scandals that had affected Boston, I felt as though I had moved to a relative oasis. But all too soon I realized that my new hometown was simply a bit delayed in examining and handling its clerical problems. Since then, the priestly scandal has exploded in the Philly (as natives call it) area.

In the wake of a grand jury report released early in 2011, then-Archbishop Justin Rigali placed twenty-one priests on leave on Ash Wednesday 2011. These priests were removed from service of all kinds and were no longer allowed to live on Church property or serve in any normal priestly capacity. This was an unexpected blow to many who had trusted the archbishop's earlier insistence that no credible accounts of abuse had been ignored; they felt compelled either to doubt the Church's prior insistence or to question the appropriateness of the abrupt removal of priests.

The large number of priests placed on leave meant that many parishes were affected. One family told me about going to three of their favorite parishes for Mass during Ash Wednesday week, only to find the usual priest missing from each. Even the most dyed-in-the-wool Catholics were emotionally and spiritually shaken. The Sunday after the announcement, Cardinal Rigali asked that a letter of explanation be read to all the parishes of the archdiocese. Our parochial vicar read it at the Mass I attended. Halfway through, he broke down in tears and did not stop weeping as he finished it.

The tears seemed to me the most honest and appropriate response I had seen thus far. How could we not weep? Priests we trusted did terrible things to trusting young people. People who should have corrected the situation promptly failed to intervene. The reputations of good priests were tarnished alongside the justly accused. The authority and reputation of a Church trying to evangelize in an often difficult environment was further weakened. And Catholics continuing to practice their faith became objects of ridicule.

Treating the Wound

Take no part in the unfruitful works of darkness, but instead expose them. — Ephesians 5:11

How much filth there is in the Church, and even among those who, in the priesthood, ought to belong entirely to him! How much pride, how much self-complacency!… The soiled garments and face of your Church throw us into confusion. Yet it is we ourselves who have soiled them! It is we who betray you time and time again, after all our lofty words and grand gestures. Have mercy on your Church….You stood up, you arose, and you can also raise us up. Save and sanctify your Church. Save and sanctify us all. — Cardinal Joseph Ratzinger (Pope Benedict XVI), Good Friday Way of the Cross, 2005

In an interview with journalist Peter Seewald, Pope Benedict XVI insisted that we "must be grateful for every disclosure [of priestly abuse]. The truth, combined with love rightly understood, is the number-one value." He insisted on this, despite the fact that for some journalists there was "pleasure in exposing the Church and if possible discrediting her."[1] Yet it is only by confronting and dealing with this pain that we can purify and serve the Church.

We start, of course, with the victims. Some suffered alone — or nearly so — with the secret of sexual abuse. Sadly, there were — and are — good reasons why the abused did not rush to tell their stories. They were so wounded by their abusers and so ashamed. Some were discouraged by attempts to tell their stories, either because they were doubted or because

---

1   Pope Benedict XVI and Peter Seewald, *Light of the World* (Ignatius: San Francisco, 2010), 27.

those listening did not recognize the intrinsic weight and horror of the wrongdoing involved. How could the Church herself be spared commensurate suffering, considering that whatever wounds humanity wounds the Church — even more so when the Church is the author of the harm?

Furthermore, now that the truth is coming to light, the Church as an institution — and each of us when called — must minister to those abused wherever and whenever we meet them.

At the same time, while there is no doubt that the "filth" in the Church has been very real, we should — despite the fear of the criticism this provokes — recognize that some aspects of the scandal are exaggerated or misrepresented. Some made false allegations against priests. Further, the Church is taking concrete steps to root out the problem — and is substantially changing those practices that allowed the problem to fester, in large part, thirty to forty years ago. Yet even if some continue to act out of bias against the Church, it is undeniably true that we do not expect priests to be "just average": they are supposed to act *in persona Christi* (representing Christ) and to be trained and educated in the ways of virtue. Priests are called "father" for a reason: they are supposed to be spiritual fathers to their parishes and parishioners. Consequently, priestly sexual abuse can take on the nature of psychological incest; it confuses the nature of a sacred relationship.[2]

---

2   A research team of the John Jay College of Criminal Justice in the City University of New York published its final report on clerical child sexual abuse (CCSA) in the Catholic Church in the United States. Prepared for the United States Conference of Catholic Bishops (USCCB) and funded by it and many Catholic and private foundations, it is titled *The Causes and Context of Sexual Abuse of Minors by Catholic Priests in the United States, 1950-2010*. It contains more information on these points.

"Simple" Solutions May Not Be So Simple

The weight of the sex-abuse scandal in the public imagination has often made us want a simple solution — fast. One of the many suggestions has been to allow clergy to marry, the idea being that this would solve the issue by providing a sexual outlet for priests. But married clergy of other faiths show a similar incidence of sexual abuse.[3] In addition, the vast majority of the abuse cases have involved adolescent males. (There were very few cases of pedophilia, a term usually reserved for the abuse of prepubescent children.) While some of this may be a consequence of a priest's greater access to boys rather than girls, in cases where it is related to same-sex attraction, having a married clergy would not likely make a difference.

A zero-tolerance policy has also been suggested: When a priest is accused of sexual abuse, he should be removed immediately. Obviously, though, such a policy would thwart our desire for justice and truth. Every accused person has not been guilty. Nor could any justice system worthy of the name so operate.

A more prudent response, given the current state of things, would include at least investigating *all* allegations *immediately* and *seriously.* This would include the Church's investigating accusations even when they are beyond the criminal statute of limitations. But, of course, it also means that not every allegation should instigate a witch hunt, which ultimately damages both the credibility of victims as well as all priests generally.

---

3   Anglican and Episcopal clergy allow married priests, as well as female ones. Their incidence of sexual abuse is very similar to that of Catholic priests. See this report on the situation with Australian Anglican clergy, for example: http://www.anglican.org.au/docs/Study%20of%20Reported%20Child%20Sexual%20Abuse%20in%20the%20Anglican%20Church%20May%202009%20Executive%20Summary.pdf

Some people have spoken likewise of opening the priesthood to females as a "cure" for the priestly scandal, since (among other reasons) women have a lower incidence of sexual abuse. But female clergy would be no quick-fix solution. Christian denominations that allow female pastors show rates of sexual abuse similar to Catholics. Further, ordaining women to the priesthood is a complex theological matter that calls for (and has received) serious independent reflection.[4] It is insufficient to treat it solely as a possible (and unproved) response to a current crisis.

There are, then, no simple solutions to the crisis, if by simple we mean "policy changes" that we could implement and then move on. Rather, the necessary changes are numerous and must affect everything from the practices and procedures used in diocesan vocation offices, seminaries, and parishes to the content of teaching at every level and institution of the Church dealing with human sexuality and priestly life, to name just a few. These are some of the new approaches suggested in the many canonical, pastoral, and administrative reflections and directives issued in response to the scandal. Many have been implemented: some at the diocesan level, and others at the national and even universal level within the Church.

Was Departure from Tradition Part of the Problem?

While the sexual abuse crisis has given rise to many criticisms of traditional Church practices, it seems that departure from Church tradition may very well be one of the sources of the

---

4   See "Embodied Ecclesiology: Church Teaching on the Priesthood" by Sister Sara Butler in Erika Bachiochi, *Women, Sex, and the Church* (Boston: Pauline, 2010), 143-159.

problem. The years in which the majority of sexual abuse took place generally coincided with the years of the sexual revolution in the wider culture, leading some to note the possibility that pieces of the sexual revolution made their way into some seminaries and dioceses.

This was also the period after the Second Vatican Council — a time of upheaval and change in the Church — when some well-intended plans had unfortunate consequences. There was a shift away from "rules" toward (often worldly) notions of "love" in the approach to Church teaching. The words of the Archbishop of Dublin help explain. Before the 1960s, he said in a conversation with Pope Benedict,

> ecclesiastical penal law functioned ... admittedly it was not perfect ... but nevertheless it was applied. After the mid-sixties, however, it was simply not applied anymore. The prevailing mentality was that the Church must not be a Church of laws but, rather, a Church of love: she must not punish. Thus the awareness that punishment can be an act of love ceased to exist. This led to an odd darkening of the mind, even in very good people."[5]

Our Role in Healing

Neither death, nor life, nor angels, nor principalities, nor things present, nor things to come, nor powers, nor height, nor depth, nor anything else in all creation, will be able to separate us from the love of God in Christ Jesus our Lord. — Romans 8:39

---

5   Seewald and Pope Benedict XVI, *Light of the World*, 25-26.

The fourteenth-century Italian writer Boccaccio wrote a story about the merchant Giannotto, who tries to convince his Jewish friend Abraham to convert to Catholicism. Eventually Abraham decides to go to Rome to check things out. When Giannotto hears this, he gives the cause up for lost, assuming that once Abraham sees the corrupt lives of the Roman clergy, he'll never convert. When Abraham returns from Rome, he continues to wish to become a Christian. Abraham explains that after seeing all manner of corruption in Rome, he is now persuaded that only the working of the Holy Spirit can account for the continued growth of the Church. He is baptized, to Giannotto's amazement and delight.

Boccaccio wrote that story for a very different era and audience, but it still rings true. Either the Church brings something new, unexpected, and humanly impossible into the world — or not. "Filth" in the Church is not something new, but the sexual-abuse scandal highlights the drama of what the Church really is — and is not. It is the continuation of Christ's presence on earth. At the same time, it is an institution composed of weak human beings, thus not free of sin and always in need of reform. Obviously, however, no matter the historical number of murderous or womanizing priests or popes, the urgency of confronting the current crisis stands.

Toward Purification and Renewal

Catholics for millennia have been proud of their membership in an institution of such historical and transcendent importance, an institution that also founded schools and hospitals, built buildings of unparalleled beauty, and served the poor. For American Catholics — who have suffered discrimination many times in the past — being part of this institution has also brought with it a kind of solidarity, a unity tied to the sense that we were part of a community that was different and misunderstood. For many, too, Catholicism is tied to an ethnic heritage.

The Church is also a refuge for many from the harshness of the culture. My husband went bowling once with a father-daughter group from our parish school. As the dads talked, one of them, referring to tuition payments, said, "I'm paying for my daughter's innocence." He expressed what many of us feel: The Church is a buffer between us and the violent, over-sexualized, selfish culture in which we live. Moreover, we look to the Church to teach us how to do the right thing and how to be better people.

But the priestly scandal has made us question this kind of belonging. We're not sure that we can be a part of this "dysfunctional" organization anymore. The evil that has happened in the Church has been so public and so shocking that it embarrasses the members of this "club." So too, when priests abuse children, we wonder how our kids can be safe. And we also wonder how, if our ordained clergy can act so wrongly, the Church can continue to be qualified to teach us to act rightly?

All these difficulties point to one hard but consequential choice: Either the Church is the place where Jesus Christ meets us in time and space, or it is not. If Jesus is not in the Church, there is no point in staying. But if this is where Jesus is present, then there is no place else to go — because there is no place where we can better find the love and mercy of Christ.

At the same time, we have to admit that we share our membership in this Church with those who have sexually abused children. But we don't and can't order any sinners out of the Church. All are offered the possibility of repentance and restitution. While few among us are child abusers, all are sinners in need of God's mercy. And many of us have committed grave sins that we may not have acknowledged even to ourselves, let alone to others. Christ knows our sinfulness, and he loves us anyway, as impossible as that seems. Just as Jesus looked at Zacchaeus and invited himself to dinner, at the Samaritan woman and knew her whole life, at the woman caught in adultery and forgave her, at the thief hanging next to him on the cross and promised him paradise — so, too, he looks at each one of us. This is the Christian paradox: Christ knows our worst sins and doesn't flinch from calling them evil, but nonetheless he loves us. He asks us to do the same, with his assistance: to acknowledge our sin, to repent and make restitution, but also to love sinners — others and ourselves.

What we need now is what we have always needed in moments of crisis: first, a truer, purer, and more authentic appreciation for Christ and the Church; and second, a commensurate commitment to renewal, which begins with making restitution to the fullest extent possible to each and every victim. Church history is replete with examples of saints and religious orders springing up to bring healing and new life in the face of the vices of the clergy and the failings and corruption of the Church.

Our problem is not how to eliminate sinners; there will always be Judases in our midst. What we need is Christian witnesses and true reform: people who are living examples of the truth of Christianity, who remind us of the higher reality to which we are all called. We need our history of renewal to repeat itself.

Beyond the Wound

Then Jesus told them a parable about their need to pray always and not to lose heart. He said, "In a certain city there was a judge who neither feared God nor had respect for people. In that city there was a widow who kept coming to him and saying, 'Grant me justice against my opponent.' For a while he refused; but later he said to himself, 'Though I have no fear of God and no respect for anyone, yet because this widow keeps bothering me, I will grant her justice, so that she may not wear me out by continually coming." And the Lord said, "Listen to what the unjust judge says. And will not God grant justice to his chosen ones who cry to him day and night? Will he delay long in helping them? I tell you, he will quickly grant justice to them." — Luke 18:1-8

Let me speak now as a woman and a mother: The scandal of priestly sexual abuse brings us to the heart of Catholic identity, an identity that we women are especially called to help retrieve and regenerate. After all, it was women who wrapped Christ's broken body in burial shrouds, and women who were the first to discover him risen and gone from the tomb.

Why women? Women have a history of treating wounds; mothers have been bandaging injuries since the beginning of time. While not all women are biological mothers, all women are called to be the "first to love" — and the Church herself is understood to be a "Mother" to all of us. There are many ways in which motherly wisdom can be a source of renewal and revitalization in the difficulties now facing us.

Mothers know that their children need to be protected from the evils of the world, many of which are beyond their understanding. We also know that our children can make serious mistakes and that sometimes it's necessary for them to be punished or suffer the consequences of their actions — not out of spite, but out of love. At the same time, they need our love and mercy despite their failings. We need to help them recognize what they have done wrong and remind them that we love them anyway. This is what we women — and Mother Church — need to do too, as painful as it is.

So, too, part of the maternal experience is an awareness of our own limits — we realize that we cannot protect our children or do as much for them as we would like. And so we pray persistently and look to models of Christian motherhood such as St. Monica, St. Augustine's mother. She never gave up on her son and prayed fervently for him her whole life, despite the many years he spent in sexual sin and away from the Church. We sometimes think of prayer as a gesture of weakness, reserved for times when there is nothing left to do. But as St. Monica demonstrates, prayer is active; it is the first kind of activism. And so today we pray for the grace of healing for the victims, as well as for our Church — for justice *and* mercy.

There is sometimes a passivity in Catholic culture that masquerades as obedience. But mothers know that true obedience is a form of loyalty — and it's anything but passive. Mothers know how to insist — gently or not — with their children. We can do the same within our Church. The great St. Catherine of Siena spent much of her short life convincing Pope Gregory IX to return to Rome from Avignon. On a certain level, we can wonder why — shouldn't the pope know that it was his job to stay in Rome as pope? Apparently, he didn't, and this man entrusted with the Church needed the many letters of Catherine in order to do the right thing. Eventually he did — he came home to Rome. In the process, Catherine became a shining example of wisdom, patience, fortitude, perseverance, and holiness for all the world to see.

We know that purification must start from within. This goes for us, our families, and our Church. Like St. Catherine, we may feel that there are truths that should be completely obvious to more people within the Church. But let's not be scandalized to the point of inaction when they are not, and instead recognize these troubles as a call to arms in the best sense — a call to constructive criticism and rebuilding, not simply accusation and recrimination, in the hope that the Church, humbled and renewed, might continue to be what she is called to be.

Rebecca Vitz Cherico received her B.A. from Yale and her Ph.D. from New York University in Spanish literature. She has taught Spanish and Humanities courses at NYU, the University of Pennsylvania, and Villanova. She is a member of the ecclesial movement Communion and Liberation and lives near Philadelphia with her husband and children.

Chapter 7

Beauty, Bounty, Balance
Avoiding the Hazards of Having

Mary Hallan FioRito, J.D.

"Ask me not what I have, but what I am."

— *Heinrich Heine, nineteenth-century*
German poet and journalist

 My husband was recently in a fender bender that, while not seriously injuring him, did destroy our 13-year-old Honda Civic. Because we both work for the Church, and we have three children enrolled in Catholic schools, we didn't have thousands of dollars sitting around waiting to be spent on a new car, nor could we assume a large car payment given our other financial obligations. So, we put out the word among friends and family that we were looking for a reliable used car.

Soon after, a classmate of mine from law school called to tell me about a colleague of his who was selling a used Lexus. It was eight years old, with 80,000 miles on it, but in good shape and very reliable. After a test drive, my husband negotiated a price with the seller that enabled us to purchase it with the cash we had received from the insurance settlement.

At first, I was thrilled. Me, driving a snazzy (albeit used) Lexus! With a CD player, a sunroof, *and* heated seats! In short order, however, I noticed that I felt extremely self-conscious, especially as I drove into the parking lot at the office, where generally everyone drives modest cars. Doubt and guilt began to creep into my thoughts: "Am I setting a bad example?" "Does this look too pretentious?" "What do people think of me, a Church employee, driving this car?" "Should I put a pro-life bumper sticker on it, or will that cause others to fall victim to the stereotype that people who oppose abortion are just rich, privileged types trying to tell poor women how many children they should have?"

I found myself quickly apologizing to anyone who asked me about my new set of wheels. "Wow, what a nice car!" someone would remark and, instead of thanking them and moving on to something important, I would find myself blurting out: "It's used! It had 80,000 miles on it! Our car was totaled, and this was all that came along!" I think that I worried a lot of my friends, who looked at me as if to say, "Um, it's a nice car. Did you have a hard day at work or something?"

I happened to mention my musings to a friend from the office, a consecrated member of Focolare, a Catholic lay movement founded during the Second World War. Women who are "consecrated" members of Focolare have lives very similar to those of female religious or nuns — they take vows of poverty and live very simply in community. My coworker seemed puzzled when I explained that I wasn't sure about driving such a luxury vehicle, even if it was eight years old. "It was a gift from God," she said to me. "Why are you not accepting it from him with joy?" Her comments reminded me that all things, even material ones, are gifts — gifts that God freely bestows on each of us.

The Hazards of Having

The incident, though, got me thinking. There are practical hazards to focusing on material things, and those are known to people of no faith or religious practice, along with those of us who seek to follow Christ. Many of us, for example, know someone who is in trouble with credit cards (or we've been in that kind of trouble ourselves). While people occasionally accumulate credit card debt because of circumstances beyond their control (like unexpected medical bills or a major appliance breakdown), often it is because they are living beyond their means. Witness the growth of shows such as *Clean House* and books such as Peter Walsh's *Enough Already!*, as well as websites such as Flylady.net (an online personal coach to manage C.H.A.O.S., aka, "Can't have anyone over syndrome"). You know that something is amiss when so many people feel that their possessions have overwhelmed them.

Equally as important as the practical hazards, however, are the moral hazards of a preoccupation with material goods. These might not be as readily apparent, but they are even more damaging because they affect us on a spiritual level, leading to selfishness and smugness, self-absorption and a callousness of heart. (Think Mr. Potter — Bedford Falls' richest yet most stingy and ruthless man in the movie *It's a Wonderful Life*.)

More to the point, I think of myself. Down what paths might I stray if I gave myself over to bigger and better and more possessions — all the choices available to me in a consumer-oriented society? I doubt that I would be free to make the choice I once saw my mother make. Nor would I ever experience the joy she experienced as a result of it.

My mother didn't work outside the home, and when my father lost his job, money was very, very tight. There were five of us under the age of ten — I was eight years old — and Christmas was approaching. My mother had all of five dollars to buy something for our Christmas stockings. Instead, knowing the need of the cloistered Carmelite nuns who lived in a monastery near our home, she sent it as an offering to them. Less than an hour after she returned from her trip to the mailbox, a friend came to the door. Her brother had just died and left her a portion of his estate. "Here's fifty dollars," she said matter-of-factly. "I'd like to give this to you for your children for Christmas."

My mother, unencumbered by a spirit of materialism, knew the things that really mattered. She gave freely — and not just from her surplus — and God rewarded her generosity and trust in him ten times over.

Her example has helped me to grapple with my own approach to possessions and money, not rejecting the world and the beautiful things in the world, but striking a balance between what my family and I need versus simply accumulating a pile of goods. Occasionally, I like to assess how I'm doing on the subject of "things" — beautiful things, expensive things, inexpensive things:

- Is this (clothing, car, furniture, home) the goal of my life? Is this what I live for?
- Do I possess my things, or do my things possess me?
- And if I'm considering buying an item: Do I need this? What difference will it make in my life?

A Balancing Act

For many Catholic women, the struggle between the love of beautiful things — furniture, clothes, jewelry, and (without delving too far into stereotypes) shoes — and the constant struggle against materialism and worldliness is a very real one. We have some examples among the saints that give us pause in this regard. St. Clare of Assisi, who cut off her luxurious golden hair (I've seen it on display among relics of her life, and it's impressive), gave up her beautiful clothes and upper-middle-class lifestyle to follow St. Francis into a radical life of poverty and prayer. And there's St. Joan of Arc who, despite being French, preferred a suit of armor to a suit from a Parisian tailor and died as a martyr for her faith.

But I feel more kinship with a fairly modern Italian saint. St. Gianna Beretta Molla was an Italian physician, wife, and mother who died in 1962. As a Catholic mother who also worked in a profession outside the home, she knew well the struggles of trying to balance her professional life, family life, and prayer life. (Her little boy was said to have been unable to sit through Mass, behaving for all of five minutes before he'd have to be removed — let's just say I can relate.) She often brought her worries home from the office, as I do more often than I care to admit.

Gianna was diagnosed with a large uterine fibroid tumor during her fourth pregnancy. She made an unselfish and courageous — yet fully conscious — decision to opt against a hysterectomy and continue with her pregnancy, even though, as a pediatrician and surgeon, she knew this could lead to the loss of her life. Without the kind of specialized medical care today's women have come to take for granted, she died of peritonitis a week after a successful cesarean delivery.

I share with St. Gianna the identical medical condition. During my first pregnancy, my doctor discovered that I had two large fibroid tumors in my uterus — as it turned out, one the size of a grapefruit and the other the size of an orange. ("You're a regular fruit basket," my obstetrician quipped.)

Many friends prayed to St. Gianna on my behalf, asking her to intercede for us for a safe delivery. On the eve of St. Gianna's feast day, I began to hemorrhage and was rushed to the hospital, where doctors safely delivered a tiny, but perfectly healthy, baby girl (whom I did not name Gianna, much to the disappointment of some, but that's a story for another day).

I'll sheepishly — but honestly — admit that, even with all of the similarities in our professional and medical situations, I feel most connected to St. Gianna because of our mutual love for stylish clothes. She is said to have told her husband, who was leaving for a business trip to Paris, to bring back a copy of the French *Vogue* magazine: "If I make it through this," she said, "I'd like to have some nice clothes after the baby is born." If women officially "sainted" by the Church can yearn for a nice new outfit from time to time, maybe clothing can garner my attention and interest from time to time, so long as it doesn't preoccupy me at the expense of really important things.

St. Gianna was not on my horizon, though, when I spent a large part of my childhood in the parish school library reading the lives of the saints, especially the female ones. Most of the women I read about — holy and virtuous and exemplary as they were — did not seem to focus on beauty, either man-made or natural, as being a gift from a good God who loves us and is the creator of all things. Those stories can leave a Catholic girl with the (wrong) impression that beauty is not something we should actively seek out, even the beauty of nature that is so evidently the work of God's hands. And as to beautiful things — there is sometimes the implication that we should actively avoid possessing them.

Of course, Scripture itself warns us about the dangers of a materialistic attitude as well as about our absolute obligation to serve Christ in the poor. These admonitions can be found throughout the Bible telling us everything from "the love of money is a root of all kinds of evil" (1 Tm 6:10) to "do not store up for yourselves treasures on earth" (Mt 6:19) to "if you wish to be perfect, go, sell your possessions, and give the money to the poor" (Mt 19:21). The late Pope John Paul II wrote more than a little about the problem of consumerism — wanting newer or more things for no reason beyond their being more new and attractive to us. He also warned us repeatedly about the dangers of rampant capitalism, cautioning even the people of his native Poland after communism fell there, and cried "foul" in countries with a wide disparity between the poor and the rich.

It is a fine line to walk, appreciating beauty and beautiful things yet recognizing that, as American women, even the poorest of us live more comfortably than most of the world's women, who worry not about whether or not they can afford another pair of strappy sandals, but rather about clean drinking water or regular meals for their children.

The Needs of My Neighbor

What are we to do? We are, of course, to practice moderation in acquiring and using possessions, but beyond that we have a more fundamental goal: detachment from those possessions. Otherwise, caught up in buying and having and guarding (not to mention repairing and dry cleaning and replacing) "things," we will be unable to hear and respond to God's invitation to follow him and serve others however those invitations come — as they will come — every day.

Detachment might sound easier than self-denial, but it is not. It is the harder but more rewarding path. If we're open to it and seeking it and attentive to those interior nudges that tell us "take this path, not that," we can develop an openhanded spirit. Free of acquisitiveness, we can put the need of our neighbor before ourselves and share not only our financial resources but all those things that are dear to us, including our time. As Chiara Lubich, the founder of the Focolare movement, noted, "We can always choose, in every moment of our life, between the way of selfishness and that of love." And love has its rewards. I know of a woman, Kathy, who understood this. Kathy had three young daughters and not much money. All three girls needed new winter coats — badly — and she'd been scouring the sales as Christmas approached, waiting for the right coats at the right price at the right moment. She finally saw a sale at a store near her home — 50 percent off, but only on a particular Saturday morning until 11 a.m. She made certain her husband would be home to watch the children so that she could be in line early, knowing the coats wouldn't last much past the doors opening.

At 8 a.m. the morning of the sale, Kathy's sister called. "It's been ages since I've seen you, and I'm going to be in the neighborhood in an hour," she said. "I'd love to stop by and spend some time with you and the kids." Kathy hesitated. She didn't see her sister often. She felt God ask her to make the sacrifice and miss the sale, but her heart was heavy when she said, "Sure, come over. I'll be here."

Kathy's sister arrived carrying a large shopping bag with an early Christmas gift for her nieces: three brand-new winter coats, even nicer than the ones Kathy had planned on purchasing at the sale. Kathy gave of herself thinking it would cost her the coats that her children really needed, but God provided for her children in a way she couldn't have imagined. Of course, Kathy didn't agree to see her sister in the hopes she'd gain from it materially. But God always sees the end of the story before we do. When we seek to honor him, by obeying his commandments and by loving others as ourselves, he meets our needs, as he promises he would do in Scripture. "Why are you anxious about clothes?" Jesus asks in St. Matthew's Gospel.

> Learn from the way the wild flowers grow. They do not work or spin. But I tell you that not even Solomon in all his splendor was clothed like one of them. If God so clothes the grass of the field, which grows today and is thrown into the oven tomorrow, will he not much more provide for you?" (Mt 6:28-30, NAB)

Sometimes, when we are generous with resources or time, we see a material and immediate blessing as Kathy did, but often we do not. Yet the nonmaterial rewards are stunning in a different way. Larry Oney, a Catholic African-American deacon serving the Church in New Orleans, is grateful for one act of generosity that helped change his life, though the woman responsible never knew the impact of her gesture. Larry was from a poor sharecropping family, and as a young child picked cotton in the rural South. His mother, determined to make better opportunities for her children, decided to move the family to New Orleans, a trip that would take them through Mississippi. Even as a small child, Larry was terrified by the prospect, knowing that, at the time, white people were hanging black people there.

They made the trip safely, however, and when Thanksgiving came, they gathered around for a meal of turnip greens and cornbread — all that they had. A knock came at the door. When they saw that it was a white woman, they thought, "If it's somebody white, it must be trouble." But she simply handed over some groceries — including a duck, an unimaginable luxury — and left. They never knew who she was. It made Larry think. "I hated all white people," he said, but now he couldn't quite reconcile his hatred with what that woman did. He was only nine years old, but "God was piercing my heart a little bit." It was the beginning of a long journey toward freedom from hatred, culminating decades later when he was baptized as a Catholic. Larry says that, to this day, he and his siblings "reflect on that duck and the bringer of that food."

Often in interviews with celebrities, reporters ask a question along the lines of "What would the forty-year-old you say to the sixteen-year-old you?" It's an interesting way to get someone to open up about what is important in life and what isn't. I've never once read any response along the lines of, "Gosh, I really should have dressed better," or "I should have worked to make more money so I could have more stuff." Rather, the answers speak of the importance of relationships over material things. Those who have experienced the sadness of losing a parent or a child talk about treasuring every possible moment with family. Others talk about the joy they have found in giving, not in receiving. Some have used their celebrity to bring attention to victims of natural disaster or a particular disease.

The entertainer Danny Thomas knew well the satisfaction that comes from helping others. Thomas founded the St. Jude Children's Research Hospital in thanksgiving for his successful career. The St. Jude website reports that when Thomas was a struggling actor and comedian with a pregnant wife, he "visited a Detroit church and was so moved during the Mass, he placed his last seven dollars in the collection box. When he realized what he'd done, Danny prayed for a way to pay the looming hospital bills. The next day, he was offered a small part that would pay 10 times the amount he'd given to the church." Thomas went on to amass incredible material wealth over the course of his career, but when he died he wasn't remembered for his fortune but for his philanthropy. It was his philanthropy, not his wealth or his talent, that led the United States Postal Service to honor him with a stamp bearing his likeness. In the end, he was judged — as we all will be — by what we do with our possessions, how we used them for the good of others.

God is never outdone in generosity, and when we give, he multiplies our efforts to accomplish his goals, whether we see it or not. And so Catholic women, wherever we find ourselves, either by circumstance or by conscious choice, can always reach out to others. In order to do this successfully, though, we need to take a measured approach to our use of this world's goods, not failing to appreciate the beauty of material things, but not allowing ourselves to be owned by them either. The woman with the new (used) Lexus, for example, has the opportunity to give an elderly parishioner a ride to the grocery store on a sub-zero-degree Chicago day. Although she still might feel guilty about driving that Lexus, even if it does have those nice heated seats.

Mary Hallan FioRito is an attorney, and the executive assistant to Francis Cardinal George, O.M.I., the Archbishop of Chicago. Formerly, she was the Archdiocese of Chicago's first Vice-Chancellor, and before that, the director of its Respect Life Office. She is married with three daughters.

Chapter 8

Who Am I? Psychology, Faith, and Same-Sex Attraction

Michelle A. Cretella, M.D.

 There is so much passion and political activism surrounding the issue of homosexuality that it is difficult to have an honest conversation about it. But I am going to attempt one, attentive both to science and faith, and with the benefit of many years as a practicing physician. Science can assist us in our search for the truth about the sources and nature of this attraction. Faith guides both our moral evaluation and personal response to individuals experiencing same-sex attraction. One additional indispensable ingredient? Humility, which allows us to approach both disciplines with the attitude of persons who have something to learn and who appreciate the need for growth personally, intellectually, spiritually. Yes, humility is an indispensible component of any honest conversation about this controversial subject.

Together, science, faith, and humility demand that my language on this subject not only accurately mirror research findings, but also reflect the compassion due every human person struggling in any way concerning sexual attraction.

Regarding compassion, this moves me to echo the words of the Catholic Church that "everyone living on the face of the earth has personal problems and difficulties, but challenges to growth, strengths, talents, and gifts as well."[1] No one, then, has a right to feel superior to those with homosexual attractions. We are all equal in human dignity and are all called to chastity. In fact, chastity, not heterosexuality, is the *virtue* to which God calls every human being. The condition of experiencing opposite-sex attraction, what we call "heterosexuality," in itself is *not* a virtue, and the condition of experiencing same-sex attraction (SSA), in itself, is *not* a sin.

To repeat then, science and faith and humility must work *together* toward a true and healthy and compassionate understanding of SSA. Science can help explain how SSA arises, but faith helps us to understand how to evaluate all sexual behavior according to the moral norm of chastity. Persons with same-sex and opposite-sex attraction are capable of unchaste behavior: sexual activity outside the freely chosen covenant of a permanent and faithful non-contracepting marriage between a man and a woman. Clearly, persons with opposite-sex attraction can also find themselves on the wrong side of this line.

To use science as a framework for considering SSA, I must clarify the use and misuse of the term "sexual orientation." As bandied about by various (claimed) experts and the media, the term is used to imply a defined identity equivalent to the identities "male" and "female." The terms heterosexual, homosexual, gay, lesbian, bisexual, queer, and transgender are similarly misused. Yet unlike one's biological sex,

---

1   "Letter to the Bishops of the Catholic Church on the Pastoral Care of Homosexual Persons," Congregation for the Doctrine of the Faith (1986), n. 16.

there is no scientific marker or medical or psychological test that distinguishes same-sex-attracted individuals from those opposite-sex-attracted. Therefore, I will primarily use the terms same-sex attraction (SSA) or "individuals with SSA," and opposite-sex attraction (OSA) or "individuals with OSA." I will also refrain from referring to homosexuality as an "illness," "disorder," or "condition," but will speak of it instead as an "adaptation" — a more scientifically correct term, and a good place to start if one's goal is to understand people experiencing this kind of attraction. Getting our scientific language right is also important for understanding how people form their moral consciences (and even their politics) regarding issues such as "same-sex marriage." For as Dr. Simon LeVay (a self-identified homosexual and researcher) noted years ago: "People who think that gays and lesbians are born that way are also more likely to support gay rights."[2]

Countless books have been written on this issue. It is impossible to adequately address homosexuality in a single chapter. Therefore, please view these pages as an invitation to travel along the road I have traveled, as a doctor and a Catholic, toward understanding both the basic elements of the science and the Catholic faith regarding same-sex attraction, as well as how science and faith fit together. It is also my hope that readers will emerge with a hunger to pursue a deeper knowledge of the divine gift of human sexuality and a greater compassion for those personally affected by SSA.

---

2   A. Dean Byrd, "In Their Own Words: Gay Activists Speak About Science, Morality, Philosophy," accessed 7/1/12 at http://narth.com/2010/09/the-innate-immutable-argument-finds-no-basis-in-science/.

I begin then with the story of how my original belief that SSA is innate and immutable led me to conclude that homosexual behavior was not an objective sin. I will then summarize what I eventually learned about behavioral science and sexual attractions, and conclude by showing how this knowledge facilitated my present view of homosexuality as a journey during which faith and science can, in synergy, lead people to claim an authentic self-identity.

The Wrestling Begins

During the early 1990s, I — like the vast majority of Americans — was led to believe that science indicated that homosexuality was a viable sexual identity. In medical school I "learned" that Drs. J. Michael Bailey, Dean Hamer, and Simon LeVay had proven that SSA was biologically determined. This is also what the mass media proclaimed to the world — even though it cannot be supported by the scientific literature. Consequently, I (like the vast majority of physicians and non-physicians alike)[3] drew the following seemingly logical conclusions:

1. If some people are born with SSA, then God made them that way.
2. If God made them that way, how can there be something sinful or "intrinsically disordered" about acting on those attractions?

---

3   Richard Friedman and Jennifer Downey, "Neurobiology and Sexual Orientation: Current Relationships," *The Journal of Neuropsychiatry & Clinical Neuroscience* 5 (1993): 131. Within their discussion these researchers state, "At clinical conferences one often hears…discussants commenting that 'homosexuality is genetic,' and, therefore, that homosexual orientation is fixed and unmodifiable. Neither assertion is true…."

3. If SSA is in a person's nature, then he or she cannot change.

4. We are supposed to be true to our nature, so those with SSA should embrace those attractions.

5. Attempting to change a person's SSA is attempting to alter their nature, and that would be harmful.

6. If others cannot accept a person's "gay" identity, then they are rejecting that person, because "gay" is who that person is.

7. Therefore, those who cannot accept a person's "gay" identity are uneducated, hateful, and/or bigoted.

Throughout my career as a medical student and a physician I had friends and mentors who identified as gay. They were kind, intelligent, creative, and loving individuals. I also encountered several gay-identified patients. One experience on the AIDS unit stands out in my mind. That is where I met Thomas and John. As my team and I walked into the room I noticed an older man sitting at Thomas' bedside with his back toward us. He clutched Thomas' hands in both of his and was hunched over Thomas' chest, quietly sobbing. His name was John. He had been Thomas' partner for 10 years. He never left Thomas' side during the hospitalization. I couldn't help but think, "This looks like love. I know sexual attractions are meant to serve reproduction. It's basic biology — our sexual bodies are designed for sexual reproduction — but ... maybe this is a normal variant of sexual behavior. Why would anyone choose this? All cases of homosexual behavior can't be wrong." Ultimately, my belief that science proved people are born gay, together with these anecdotal experiences, led to my rejection of the Church's teaching on homosexuality for the first six years of my medical career.

One day a patient revealed that a colleague of mine, Dr. V., had given him a brochure about a local chapter of Courage. Courage is a ministry of the Catholic Church that offers support to Catholics experiencing SSA and desiring to live a chaste lifestyle in accordance with Church teaching. It is a ministry similar to that of Alcoholics Anonymous. I was dismayed that a fellow doctor — particularly one as seemingly compassionate as my friend — would promote an organization that I believed forced people to deny who they really are. How could she be so "unscientific" and cruel? She was used to that sort of confrontation. She smiled when I asked her to explain her position and replied, "It's not like that. If you actually go to the literature yourself you will see that we were misled. Hamer, LeVay, and the others never claimed or proved that homosexuality is inborn. Besides, the last time I checked, I exist, though the media imply that people like me do not." That's when my colleague — a mother of two and married for more than twenty-five years — shocked me further by explaining that she had had same-sex attractions between the ages of four and eighteen; by age eighteen the attractions and fantasies had abated.

I didn't know what to say or believe at that moment. My friend had nothing to gain from lying. Yet, every medical and mental-health organization maintained then as they do now that homosexuality is a normal sexual variant and essentially unchangeable. How could organized medicine and psychology be wrong?

Same-Sex Science and the Politics of Truth

In 2005 Dr. Nicholas Cummings, a past president of the American Psychological Association, co-published the book *Destructive Trends in Mental Health: The Well-Intentioned Path to Harm.* Dr. Cummings explains that while he agrees homosexuality is not a mental illness, when "the American Psychiatric Association yielded suddenly and completely to political pressure ... in 1973," by "removing homosexuality as a treatable ... condition," it was because a "political firestorm had been created by gay activists within psychiatry." Intense opposition had come from only a "few outspoken psychiatrists who were [consequently] demonized and even threatened, rather than scientifically refuted. Psychiatry's House of Delegates sidestepped the conflict by putting the matter to a [nonrepresentative[4]] vote of the membership, marking the first time in the history of health care that a diagnosis or lack of diagnosis was decided by popular vote rather than by scientific evidence."[5]

Dr. Cummings personally introduced two resolutions to normalize homosexuality within the American Psychological Association in 1974, but did so with the stipulation that "appropriate and needed research would be conducted to substantiate these decisions."[6] The resolutions passed. He then watched — for decades — "with dismay as there was no effort on the part of the APA to promote or even encourage such

---

4   Jeffrey Satinover, *Homosexuality and the Politics of Truth* (Grand Rapids, MI: Baker Books, 1996), 31-35.

5   Rogers Wright and Nicholas Cummings, eds., *Destructive Trends in Mental Health* (New York: Routledge, 2005), 9. See also "This American Life" by WBEZ, originally aired on Public Radio International January 18, 2002 (accessed on 6/30/12 from www.thisamericanlife.org/radio-archives/episode/204/81-words)

6   Ibid.

required research. *The two APAs had established forever that medical and psychological diagnoses are subject to political fiat*"[7] [emphasis mine]. Following the American Psychiatric Association's and the American Psychological Association's nonscientific response to the issue, nearly all other medical organizations eventually followed suit.[8]

Is Heterosexual Attraction Inborn?

Perhaps the best way to begin understanding SSA is to examine what we know about the development of OSA. Dr. Neil Whitehead, in his book *My Genes Made Me Do It*, summarizes the psychosexual literature that reveals that heterosexual attraction is closely linked to the formation of gender identification. It appears, in other words, that heterosexuality is learned over a period of time as a response to a variety of environmental factors and unique experiences. These factors include a strong bond with the mother from infancy through the first few years of life. This bond develops the ability to experience the affection of — or show affection to — those of the same and opposite sex. Later, somewhere between the ages of two-and-a-half to four years of age, the child begins to identify with and imitate the same-sex parent.

Healthy gender identification is further enhanced by being accepted by same-sex siblings and peers, as well as identifying with them. Through healthy family and same-sex peer interactions, children also come to identify and subconscious-

---

7   Ibid.

8   To access websites of scientific, secular, and faith-based organizations that support an individual's right to attempt to alter their same-sex attractions and/or to embrace a celibate lifestyle, visit Positive Alternatives To Homosexuality at www.pathinfo.org.

ly assimilate what is culturally accepted as masculine or feminine traits and behaviors. Around the time of puberty, the release of hormones adds sexual drive to the prevailing gender identity, and boys and girls who are secure in their own masculinity and femininity then take an interest in the opposite sex.[9] In short, while we are born male or female and capable of a sexual response, we are not born with pre-wired heterosexual attractions — these develop over time.[10]

Is SSA Innate?

From where did the claim arise, then, that SSA is "innate"? Only from activists, never scientists. In fact, during the last forty years, even while the majority of SSA studies have been conducted, reviewed, and published by SSA-affirming researchers — many of whom openly identify as homosexual (and are thus unlikely to deny or diminish the significance of biological factors) — every study has failed to prove that SSA is inborn. This is so despite the extensive varieties of approaches employed, from gene analysis to brain structure, fingerprint styles, handedness, finger lengths, eye blinking, ear characteristics, verbal skills, and prenatal hormones.[11] This includes the widely publicized twin studies of Dr. Michael J. Bailey, the brain research of Dr. Simon LeVay, and the gay

9   Neil E. Whitehead, *My Genes Made Me Do It!* (2010), 266, available at www.mygenes.co.nz/download.htm (accessed June 14, 2012).

10   Ibid., 103-112. There is not enough space to discuss the topic of "Disorders of Sexual Differentiation" resulting in persons sometimes referred to as "intersex" or "hermaphrodites." Dr. Neil Whitehead, however, explains how research in this area also supports the importance of environmental and social influences in shaping sexual attractions over that of biological factors.

11   Michelle Cretella, "Empowering Parents of Gender Discordant and Same-Sex Attracted Children," Position Statement of the American College of Pediatricians, nos. 3-7, accessed July 1, 2012, at www.acpeds.org/Empowering-Parents-of-Gender-Discordant-and-Same-Sex-Attracted-Children.html.

gene research of Dr. Dean Hamer — the very same research that I was taught (and the media claims) proves SSA to be biologically determined. Instead, all three researchers have stated the very opposite.

In 1996, for example, Dr. Hamer, when asked if homosexuality is solely biologically rooted said, "Absolutely not. From twin studies, we already know that half or more of the variability in sexual orientation is not inherited. Our studies try to pinpoint the genetic factors ... not negate the psychosocial factors."[12] In the most succinct summary of the research on genetics and SSA, Dr. Francis Collins, the former director of the National Human Genome Research Institute and the current director of the National Institutes of Health, wrote:

> The likelihood that the identical twin of a homosexual male will also be gay is about 20 percent (compared with 2-3 percent of males in the general population), indicating that sexual orientation is genetically influenced but *not hardwired by DNA*, and that whatever genes are involved represent predispositions, not predeterminations" [emphasis mine].[13]

Simply stated, identical twins share 100 percent of their genetic material and develop in identical prenatal environments, exposed to the same types and levels of prenatal hormones in their mother's uterus. Therefore, if SSA were completely genetic, or if it were due solely to the influence of prenatal hormones, then when one identical twin has SSA, the other twin would also. But this is not the case.

---

12   Anastasia Toufexis and Alice Park, "New evidence of a gay gene." Time (November 13, 1995), 43.

13   Francis Collins, *The Language of God* (New York: Free Press, 2006), 260.

What Does Cause SSA?

The development of SSA best fits a risk-factor model rather than a simplified "If A then B" model. For example, there is evidence that sexual abuse is a risk factor that can contribute to developing SSA. This does not mean that sexual abuse unilaterally causes SSA: Not all children who are sexually abused will develop SSA, and not every individual with SSA experienced childhood sexual abuse. However, for many individuals with unwanted SSA, childhood sexual abuse was one of the factors that contributed. In the words of my colleague Dr. V.:

> There is no one cause of SSA; it is never one thing. It is always a combination of many factors — usually including personality traits — plus one or more wounds, social factors, and life choices (such as whether or not to view pornography, masturbate, experiment sexually with others, join a pro-gay organization, and so forth). The wounds that lead to SSA for any given individual may be "objective" or "subjective" (that is, innocent actions *perceived as hurtful* by the individual). The wounds may be due to obvious traumas like sexual abuse or rape. Other times the wounds may be much less obvious because they occurred during infancy and early childhood, disrupting the bond between mother and child, or father and child. This is why many with SSA say, "I always felt different. I had to be born this way."
>
> Other times the wounds are inflicted by peers who ostracize the artistic, less athletic boys, for example. Possibly the most hurtful wounds are inflicted by people of faith who find homosexual behavior to be immoral, then go on to deride those with SSA and those they perceive to be SSA. Again, wounds alone do not determine SSA, but typically contribute in a significant way. Every person with SSA has his or her own unique story.

There is scientific evidence from at least three different psychological frameworks — the psychoanalytic, social learning, and interactional theories — to support Dr. V.'s explanation. The psychoanalytical literature indicates that homosexuality emerges from a context of difficult family relationships, particularly a disconnected father and an over-involved mother. Alternatively, there may be a disruption in the mother-infant bonding. The resulting unhealthy relationships contribute to the child's rejection of a masculine or feminine gender identity and may lead to SSA just prior to or during puberty.[14]

Social learning theory explains how individuals learn through experiences and observations and by adopting actions and attitudes from significant others. It maintains that behavioral conditioning, both direct and indirect, accounts for attractions we develop and the behaviors we adopt. From this perspective, children and adolescents learn about sexual behavior and sexual preference from parents, peers, and the media. They are rewarded or punished by significant others for their sexual attitudes and behaviors.[15] Social learning theory also accounts for the role of serious trauma, such as sexual abuse, in the development of SSA. Some researchers have observed a higher prevalence of sexual abuse in the histories of both male and female homosexuals. This is well-established in the literature, yet little known by the public.[16]

---

14   Douglas A. Abbott and A. Dean Byrd, *Encouraging Heterosexuality* (Utah: Millennium Press, 2011), 27-29.

15   Ibid., 29.

16   Ibid., 30-31. For example, Shrier and Johnson found that boys who were sexually abused were seven times more likely to identify as homosexual or bisexual. Tomeo, Templer, Anderson, and Kotler noted that 46 percent of gay men and 22 percent of gay women were sexually abused as children, compared with only 7 percent of matched heterosexual men and 1 percent of matched heterosexual women.

There is also evidence from the social-learning litera-ture to support the role of peers in the development of SSA. The research suggests that a lack of connection with same-sex peers sets the stage for later development of SSA. Young men experiencing peer neglect or peer abuse, such as teasing and bullying, often feel disconnected from their own masculin-ity. Such trauma, particularly during the early pre-adolescent years, can cause gender confusion.[17]

While many with unwanted SSA do fall into the psycho-analytic or social-learning frameworks, others do not. Conse-quently, Dr. Daryl C. Bem developed the interactional theory that combines the indirect or predisposing effects of biology with environmental factors to explain SSA. Put simply, the interactional theory postulates that biologically predisposed personality traits are nurtured in relationships and environ-mental contexts that result in the development of SSA.[18]

As previously noted, the American Psychological Asso-ciation (APA) has long been dominated by gay-affirming psy-chologists. Significantly, however, even the APA has moved away from its 1998 emphasis upon the potential biological causes of homosexuality to its 2008 statement:

> Although much research has examined the possible genetic, hormonal, developmental, social, and cultural influences on sexual orientation, no findings have emerged that permit sci-entists to conclude that sexual orientation is determined by any particular factor or set of factors. *Many think that nature and nurture both play complex roles*; most people experience

---

17   A. Dean Byrd, "Same-Sex Marriage and the Schools: Potential Impact on Children Via Sexuality Education," Brigham Young University Education and Law Journal 2 (2011), 186.

18   Ibid., 187, and Abbott and Byrd (2009), 33.

little or no sense of choice about their sexual orientation [emphasis mine].[19]

One further general but important scientific perspective on SSA: It is a well-accepted scientific fact that complex behavior traits regularly involve the interaction of multiple genes with multiple environmental factors, plus *free-will choices*. Why would SSA and its associated behaviors be different? In fact they are not. That is why it is accurate to say both that sexual attractions are generally not chosen, but that responses to those attractions do involve choice. Unbidden attractions may come because of situational factors and prior sexual experiences. There may be a biological predisposition that makes such attractions more likely than not. However, these attractions may be increased or decreased by the choices that people make. The medical term for this dynamic is a "biopsychosocial model mediated by choice." This newer model is what the best research on homosexuality appears to reflect.[20] It is also well-illustrated by Dr. V.'s personal experience described here:

I did not choose my same-sex attractions. They developed by the time I was only four years old. I was raised in a loving family, never suffered any form of sexual or other abuse, and was as feminine as a girl can be. However, my father verbally abused my mother; he constantly put her down and limited her ability to develop friendships. Because of this she was not as emotionally available to me as I needed her to be. I

---

19   American Psychological Association, "Sexual Orientation and Homosexuality: Answers to Your Questions for a Better Understanding of Sexual Orientation and Homosexuality" (Washington, D.C.: APA, 2008), available at http://www.apa.org/topics/sexuality/orientation.aspx; cf. A. Dean Byrd, "APA's New Pamphlet on Homosexuality De-emphasizes the Biological Argument, Supports a Client's Right to Self-Determination," available at www.narth.com/docs/deemphasizes.html.

20   Abbott and Byrd (2009), 47-52.

frequently comforted her.... I was also extremely shy and had very little interest in playing with other children [psychoanalytic theory: "the mother wound," temperament, and estrangement from peers].

Also, at the same age, I recall my mother sponge bathing me and experiencing that as pleasurable. There was nothing inappropriate about what my mother did, but my perception of this experience imprinted on my mind. I associated that touch and the pleasurable feelings with safety and comfort well before I ever knew about what sexual touch was, and this led to desires and fantasies about other attractive women my mother's age [social-learning theory].

Around age thirteen I decided that these feelings and fantasies were not normal. For me it was Biology 101 — sex is first and foremost about making babies. I wanted to get married and have children someday. A "gay" lifestyle did not fit into my worldview. I decided to stop the thoughts the moment they entered my mind, commit to chastity, and see what would happen [she exercised her moral agency]. This decision plus an adventitious strengthening of my relationship with my mother, the development of new friendships that prompted me to be more outgoing, and the fact that there were no gay activist student groups in my high school allowed me to be free from SSA by the age of eighteen [interactional model mediated by choice].

Is SSA Changeable? And If So, How Changeable Is It?

Many will be surprised to learn that success rates for change of orientation are in the same range of success rates for treating other similar behavioral challenges. Author and self-described pagan lesbian Camille Paglia has perhaps summarized it best: "Sexuality is highly fluid, and reversals theoretically possible. However, habit is refractory, once the sensory pathways have been blazed and deepened by repetition — a phenomenon obvious in the struggle with obesity, smoking, alcoholism, or drug addiction."[21]

Before 1973, when lobbying by gay activists led to the removal of homosexuality from the psychiatric manual, psychological care was routinely provided to those with unwanted SSA. In reviewing the research prior to this time, Dr. Jeffrey Satinover reported a composite success rate of 50 percent.[22] Dr. Neil Whitehead also noted that these success rates are within the same range as success rates for treating drug and alcohol addiction.[23]

Research from the last decade by Drs. Lisa Diamond, Ellen Schecter, Elan Karten, Mark Yarhouse, and others continues to demonstrate the fluidity of sexual attractions.[24] Gay-rights supporter and past APA president Dr. Cummings recently spoke of his 20 percent success rate with clients with unwanted SSA in his private practice.[25]

Finally, I would be remiss not to mention Robert Spitzer's study published in 2003. Despite his "apology" to the gay community for publishing it,[26] there has been no new data to contradict his original results. Dr. Spitzer's research

---

21   Camille Paglia, *Vamps & Tramps*, (New York: Vintage, 1994), 78.

22   Satinover, *Homosexuality and the Politics of Truth*, 186.

23   Whitehead, *My Genes Made Me Do It!* 248.

24   Byrd, "Same-Sex Marriage and the Schools: Potential Impact on Children Via Sexuality Education," 190.

25   Joseph Nicolosi, "Former APA President Interviewed at 2011 NARTH Convention," accessed July 1, 2012, at http://josephnicolosi.com/interviews.

26   Benedict Carey, "Psychiatry Giant Sorry for Backing Gay 'Cure,'" Health Section, New York Times (May 18, 2012), accessed July 1, 2012, at www.nytimes.com/2012/05/19/health/dr-robert-l-spitzer-noted-psychiatrist-apologizes-for-study-on-gay-cure.html?pagewanted=all.

remains scientifically sound, and his original conclusion — that some highly motivated individuals with unwanted SSA can change — still stands.[27] This is why Dr. Kenneth Zucker, editor of the *Archives of Sexual Behavior*, refused to print a retraction of the study.

It is important to know that it was Dr. Spitzer who was instrumental in declassifying homosexuality as a mental disorder in 1973. For thirty years he believed that change of orientation was impossible. After interviewing 200 self-identified ex-gays, however, he found that every participant had experienced some degree of change as well as other positive outcomes such as improved self-esteem. Sixty-six percent of the men and forty-four percent of the women reported experiencing good heterosexual functioning. None experienced harm.[28] But after his study was published, Dr. Spitzer was the object of intense discrimination and harassment not only from gay activists, but also from those he had considered professional colleagues and friends; all for publishing a politically incorrect but scientific study.[29]

Homosexuality as an Adaptation, Not an Identity

Despite the anger one might feel about the failure of both the scientific community and the media to allow the facts about SSA to come forward, our response as Catholics to persons

---

27   Christopher Rosik, "Spitzer's 'Retraction': What Does It Really Mean?" (June 1, 2012), accessed July 1, 2012, at http://narth.com/2012/06/2532/.

28   Robert L. Spitzer, "Can Some Gay Men and Lesbians Change Their Sexual Orientation? 200 Participants Reporting a Change from Homosexual to Heterosexual Orientation," Archives of Sexual Behavior 32 (2003): 403, 413.

29   Douglas Leblanc, "Therapeutically Incorrect," Christianity Today (March 29, 2005) accessed July 1, 2012, at www.christianitytoday.com/ct/2005/april/20.94.html. (Also view NARTH's commentary on this interview accessed July 2, 2012, at www.narth.com/docs/spitzerct.html.)

with SSA must proceed from the same principles that guide all of our Catholic behavior: love, in truth. As Dr. V. said:

> No one has a right to feel superior to those with SSA, and certainly no right to harass or abuse them. We are all wounded in some way. It is an inescapable part of being human. That is why Christ died for us — so that we would have hope: hope for healing and, more importantly, the hope of everlasting life.

Christians know that we are all disordered in some way; it is a part of the human condition because each of us enters his world with the stain of original sin. Baptism frees us of the guilt associated with this sin but does not fully heal us. Also, our "wound" predisposes us to inflict wounds upon each other. Throughout our lives, as outlined in the scientific literature above, we adapt to these subsequent wounds according to our biologically influenced temperaments, the environment in which we are nurtured, and the choices we make. Some developmental adaptations are healthful and some are not. The term "adaptations" as opposed to "disorders" is important. It allows for a more scientifically based as well as more open and honest dialogue not only about SSA, but also about all mental and behavioral health challenges.

How does the science of SSA that we know thus far and the Church's affirmation of the universal fact of original sin interact with Catholic teaching on our human sexuality and its expression? The *Catechism of the Catholic Church* teaches that every individual must "acknowledge and accept his sexual *identity*." This refers to the "physical, moral, and spiritual *difference* and *complementarity*" of both genders, which are "oriented toward the goods of marriage and the flourishing of family life" (see No. 2333). This is an identity rooted in our being made in the image of God — God who is three persons, living in constant, complete, and fruitful loving communion, as men and women are capable of complete and fruitful loving communion.

The *Catechism* admonishes us to reject the reductionist identification of a person by reference solely to his or her sexual orientation. There are spiritual, relational, physical, emotional, and mental costs to claiming and acting upon this false identity. Spiritually, the Church explains that, "As in every moral disorder, homosexual activity prevents one's own fulfillment and happiness by acting contrary to the creative wisdom of God. The Church, in rejecting erroneous opinions regarding homosexuality, does not limit personal freedom and dignity realistically and authentically understood."[30]

To the extent that it can (as it lacks the competence for moral conclusions), science complements Catholic teaching here. It shows how acting on SSA is a risk factor for significant medical and psychological illnesses that prevent fulfillment, happiness, and the exercise of personal freedom.[31]

This is a badly needed context for considering the fullness of the human person. No one is reduced merely to the label of a "heterosexual" or a "homosexual." Rather, all are creatures of God. Each struggles with inborn and acquired difficulties but is also blessed with God's grace and called to respond as a child of God and as an heir to eternal life.[32] There

---

30   "Some Considerations Concerning the Response to Legislative Proposals on the Non-Discrimination of Homosexual Persons," Congregation for the Doctrine of the Faith (July 22, 1992), 3.

31   Philip M. Sutton, ed., "A Discussion of Specific Areas of Medical and Mental Health Risk," *Journal of Human Sexuality 1* (2009), 57-87.

32   "Letter to the Bishops of the Catholic Church on the Pastoral Care of Homosexual Persons," Congregation for the Doctrine of the Faith (1986), 16.

is real relief — psychological and spiritual — in adopting the Catholic perspective. David Prosen, a therapist and former homosexual, explains that "by defining myself as a 'gay' male, I had taken on a false identity.... One *is not* a same-sex attraction, but instead *experiences* this attraction."[33] Dr. Gerard van den Aardweg, a psychoanalyst who has helped hundreds of men distressed by unwanted SSA, adds:

> [It is a] psychologically dangerous *decision* to identify oneself as a different species of man: 'I *am* a homosexual.'... It may give a sense of relief after a period of struggle and worry, but at the same time it is defeatist.... The self-identified homosexual takes on the [tragic] role of the definitive outsider.... That role brings certain rewards.... It makes one feel at home among fellow homosexuals. It temporarily takes away the tension of having to fight homosexual impulses and yields the *emotional gratifications of feeling unique and tragic* — and, of course, of having sexual adventures.... Real happiness, let alone inner peace, is never found that way. Restlessness will increase, as will the feeling of an inner void. Conscience will send out its disquieting and persistent signals. For it is a false 'self' the unhappy person has identified with.... Initially, it is a seducing dream; in time it turns out to be a terrible illusion ... leading an unreal life, ever farther away from one's real person [self]"[34] (emphasis in original).

---

    33   David Prosen, "I am Not Gay ... I am David," *Lay Witness Magazine* (January/February 2011).

    34   Gerard Van den Aardweg, *Battle for Normality: Self-Therapy for Homosexual Persons* (San Francisco: Ignatius, 1997), 20.

Dr. V., based on her own experience, states:

The Church is correct: No one is forced to claim a gay identity. Sexual attractions are one part of a person; they do not define the person. SSA is not chosen, but *chastity is a choice*: Change of sexual attractions followed by marriage is possible; others joyfully embrace a celibate life. Contrary to popular belief, human beings can live happy and fulfilling lives without sex. It is love that we can't live without.

So how can we love those with SSA without affirming their SSA? The very same way we love anyone else: through friendship and prayer. True friends appreciate each other's unique gifts and acknowledge one another's identity as the man or woman God created them to be. Through friendship, men and women with same-sex attraction will gain the experiential knowledge that they are loved by us, and together we might gain a glimpse of the love of God.

Michelle A. Cretella, M.D., has practiced as a board-certified pediatrician for fifteen years caring for children from infancy through young adulthood. She is the vice president of the American College of Pediatricians and serves on the board of directors of the National Association for Research and Therapy of Homosexuality. She and her husband have four children.

Chapter 9

The Single Mother
Threading the Needle

Helen M. Alvaré, J.D., M.A.

 A unique collection of forces buffets the single mother today. In a world where almost anything goes as far as sex is concerned, she still draws significant moral disapproval from the U.S. public, according to recent surveys. Furthermore, a vast number of social scientists today find themselves in rare agreement regarding the disadvantages to children growing up in a single-parent home. And perhaps most amazing of all, social science is confirming Catholic sexual morality concerning nonmarital sexual relations.

This is a rare alignment and merits attention, not only because of what adults owe innocent children, but also because the flourishing of women and of society is closely tied to getting marriage and motherhood right. There are even more and sometimes confusing considerations for the single mother who is Catholic, or who comes into close contact with Catholic circles:

- While this Church is very closely associated with the message of moral disapproval of nonmarital sexual relationships, it is also perhaps the most likely to offer copious outreach to women experiencing nonmarital pregnancies.

- It is further extremely closely associated with urging women to welcome and celebrate every new life, no matter their circumstances.
- It is also the largest private provider of services to the poor (and single motherhood is one of the top indicators for poverty).

There is also the fact, of course, of the Catholic faith's unique dedication to motherhood as a vocation. The most famous human being in all of Catholicism, let's not forget, is a young woman who said yes to motherhood in circumstances socially embarrassing to her at the time: Mary, the Mother of God.

How is a single mother to comprehend all of this? Not only in regard to herself, but also as a woman who hopes that, no matter her situation, her own children might experience parenting in the best possible way? And how can Catholics reflect on and act in both love and truth regarding this phenomenon?

These are tricky questions, but after spending more than a year and a half reading and writing on the subject in my capacity as a professor who thinks about the intersection of religion and social policy, I will venture to address them. During that time of immersion, I read everything that was credible and available in the social sciences and legal literature — and a lot of popular literature too — on nonmarital births.[1] (This

---

1   *See e.g.* Kathryn Edin and Maria Kefalas, *Promises I Can Keep: Why Poor Women Put Motherhood Before Marriage* (Berkley, CA; University of California Press, 2005); Paula England and Kathryn Edin, *Unmarried Couples with Children* (New York: Russell Sage Foundation, 2007); Margaret K. Nelson, *The Social Economy of Single Motherhood: Raising Children in Rural America* (Oxford, UK: Routledge, 2005); Judith Musick, *Young, Poor, and Pregnant: The Psychology of Teen Motherhood* (New Haven,

field of research bumps up against that of single motherhood because women, by about a 9-to-1 ratio with men, are the persons who most often parent children born outside of a marriage.) I was stunned by the frequency of nonmarital births in the teeth of all that is known about their associated disadvantages for women and for children: They are a bit more than four out of every ten births in the United States today. I also felt both overwhelmed for and compassionate toward the women and girls caught up in the vortex of to-day's sex and mating markets, especially those women and girls who are less socially privileged. I came to better understand women's drive for human communion and the very modern and practical difficulties of satisfying this drive at the level of the "gold standard" — that is, in the context of a stable marriage with a man who recognizes the full measure of a woman's dignity. Finally, I wanted to help women and men understand the sacredness of both sexes' obligations to children, even before conception. Talk about threading the needle!

My conclusions, related here in nearly criminally brief fashion, are as follows[2]: First, none of us should be exempt from a strong dose of the facts about the difficulties of single parenting, neither rich nor poor, black nor white, newly immigrated or longtime citizen. Ignoring the facts in the name of "compassion" is no true compassion. Even (by which, of course, I mean to imply ironically, "in particular") feminists

---

CT: Yale University Press, 1993); Christine Coppa, *Rattled! A Memoir* (New York: Broadway Books, 2009); *Motherlode*, http://parenting.blogs.nytimes.com; *Black Moms Club*, http:blackmomsclub.ning.com.

2   My lengthier scholarship on the subject can be found at "Beyond the Sex-Ed Wars: Addressing Disadvantaged Single Mothers' Search for Community," *Akron Law Review 44* (2011): 167.

long wary of marriage need to attend to this if they care about women's equality and freedom in the long run.

Second, no one should be exempt from learning — as best we can — *why* the phenomenon of single parenting is galloping along today at such a rate. To condemn, as so many do, but not to get the facts, and not to empathize, gets all of us nowhere, and gets some of us angry enough to tune out true and salutary messages about the goods of parenting with an involved father in a stable marriage. Further, it betrays a real thickheadedness to fail to understand why a woman might actively want a baby to love, or why she would be willing to carry to term even a pregnancy perceived to be a crisis. How can we help her or her children if we don't understand?

Third and finally, it would be great — especially since the leading actor in this field today (government) is getting things so horridly wrong about *why* single motherhood is growing and *how* it should respond — for the Church to get it right. Every once in a while, government or quasi-state actors such as the National Campaign to Prevent Teen and Unplanned Pregnancy realize that their efforts are not getting the job done, and they plead for religious involvement. But in my view, there hasn't yet been a sufficiently large or on-target religious response. The Church should, therefore, not only continue to welcome every human person (in Pope Benedict XVI's inimitable words) with that "look of love which they crave,"[3] but also speak more often and more creatively about the importance of linking sex with children conceived in marriage.

3   Pope Benedict XVI, *Deus Caritas Est*, encyclical letter (www.vatican.va, 2005), 18.

Newsflash: Religion and Social Science on the Same Page?!

These days, negative news about single parenting is everywhere. *Coming Apart*, a respected 2012 book by sociologist Charles Murray, for example, summarized the situation as follows:

> No matter what the outcome being examined — the quality of the mother-infant relationship, externalizing behavior in childhood (aggression, delinquency, and hyperactivity), delinquency in adolescence, criminality as adults, illness and injury in childhood, early mortality, sexual decision-making in adolescence, school problems and dropping out, emotional health, or any other measure of how well or poorly children do in life — the family structure that produces the best outcomes for children, on average, is two biological parents who remain married.... All of these statements apply after controlling for the family's socioeconomic status.[4]

Other respected expert sources have reached the same conclusion.[5] One study determined, for example, that "an extensive body of research tells us that children do best when they grow up with both biological parents in a low-conflict marriage." A June 2012, nationally representative, and widely hailed family-structures study points in the same direction. The author concluded that his "New Families Structure Survey":

---

4 Charles Murray, *Coming Apart: The State of White America, 1960-2010* (New York: Crown, 2012), 158. (citations omitted).

5 See e.g. Kristin Anderson Moore, Susan M. Jekielek, and Carol Emig, "Marriage from a Child's Perspective: How Does Family Structure Affect Children and What Can We Do About It?" Child Trends Research Brief (www.childtrends.org/files/marriagerb602.pdf, June 2002).

clearly reveals that children appear most apt to succeed well as adults — on multiple counts and across a variety of domains — when they spend their entire childhood with their married mother and father, and especially when the parents remain married to the present day. Insofar as the share of intact, biological mother/father families continues to shrink in the United States, as it has, this portends growing challenges within families, but also heightened dependence on public health organizations, federal and state public assistance, psychotherapeutic resources, substance-use programs, and the criminal justice system.[6]

Surprisingly, this may still come as news to a wide variety of Americans who aren't breathlessly following family sociology trends the way some professors do (guilty). Further, many might still remember the frequent public speculation that money could close the gap between single-parent families and married families. (Such speculation occurred more in the past, but is still with us today courtesy, largely, of some pretty ideological interest groups and academics.) Especially in the 1970s and '80s, there was a lot of blather to the effect that new family forms could provide the same beneficial outcomes for children and might even provide superior happiness for adults. Leading feminist groups pushed the line that women in particular might well be happier without marriage, given the "patriarchal" arrangements they claimed were inescapably associated with the institution.

Another factor in downplaying the importance of marriage was probably in play here too: a desire to avoid appear-

---

6   Mark Regnerus, "How Different Are the Adult Children of Parents Who Have Same-Sex Relationships? Findings from the New Family Structures Study," *Social Science Research* 41 (2012): 752, 766.

ing racist or anti-poor. This factor remains today, but it was particularly evident in the 1970s and '80s due to an emerging awareness that disadvantaged Americans — including some African-Americans and those who were at the bottom of the income scales — were single-parenting at increasingly high rates. There arose an apparently strong desire to appear nonjudgmental respecting each of these groups, especially in the era immediately following the passage of civil rights laws. Writings abounded claiming that the disadvantages associated with single parenting were strictly a function either of the legacy of slavery or, for all races, of poverty, and that generously funded government welfare programs were the answer. But the period from the 1990s to today brought a flood of studies indicating that this position could no longer be maintained. A lack of money could account for some, but not more than half, of the disadvantage to children reared in single-parent homes. The lack of a second, married parent, with all that means for the family system, is itself significant.[7]

It appears then that we cannot avoid confronting the fact that there is something about having a mother and a father in a stable, committed relationship that matters. Just to put this on paper is to perceive its truth. How could it *not* matter to children that their mother has the support of their father and vice versa? That when one adult is at the end of his or her rope, the child has a second adult to whom he or she can turn? That women and men bring different and sometimes complementary strengths to the parenting enterprise?

---

7   Sara MacLanahan, "The Consequences of Single Motherhood, in Sex, Preference and Family," *Essays on Law and Nature*, 306, 310 (David M. Estlund and Martha C. Nussbaum, eds., New York: Oxford University Press, 1998).

That one's genetic inheritance and extended family is securely known versus unknown?

Yet to say all of these things is only the first step. Unless we better understand the mind of the single woman on these matters, we can only nod our heads in agreement with the data. We can't speak to her in a way that will convince her to think in advance — before conception — about where her own happiness and freedom, or those of her children, lie.

The Thinking of the Single Woman Who Becomes a Mother: Why Does She Do It?

It is no secret that the woman holds the key to the decision "yes" or "no" when it comes to consensual, nonmarital sex. In other words, the economics and psychology professors who call women the "sellers" and men the "buyers" in the market for nonmarital sex do so for good reason.[8] Sociologists, via the results of extensive surveys, describe the elements of this phenomenon, reporting for example that men desire and obtain more sexual partners than women over a lifetime and are more likely to initiate sexual encounters than are women.

So why does a single woman risk becoming a single mother? Why does she engage in sex without a commitment between her and the man (whether she hopes actively to avoid a baby, or is sort of willing to have one, or even seeks a child)? It would be impossible to answer fully in this brief space, but I will attempt a summary. To try to find out during my year-and-a-half of research, I spent a lot of time immersed in what

---

8   See e.g. Roy F. Baumeister and Kathleen D. Vohs, "Sexual Economics: Sex as Female Resource for Social Exchange in Heterosexual Interactions," *Personality and Social Psychology Review 8* (2004) 339.

is called the "qualitative" literature about single moms. This is the literature reporting what limited groups of women said at some length to researchers about what they were thinking. I read about urban and rural women, about upper-middle-class, middle-class and poor women. I read in the areas of law, sociology, and psychology, among other relevant disciplines.[9]

Again, simplifying drastically for the purposes of this chapter, I came to this very broad conclusion: People long for loving companionship — even stronger, *communion* — with another person. This is well put at a very fundamental level by John Cacioppo, coauthor of the book *Loneliness: Human Nature and the Need for Social Connection*.[10] He comments that it is so well known that human companionship is essential to human happiness that solitary confinement has been designated the penultimate punishment meted out for crimes (with capital punishment, of course, being the ultimate). He also describes studies showing that when people experience loneliness, their judgment and even their cognitive abilities can become impaired. The literature on self-reported "happiness" indicates similarly and goes further to suggest that people are, on average, happier in more deeply committed romantic relationships (marriage) than with less committed relationships (cohabitation) or without such a relationship at all (divorced or single).

How does this longing for communion factor into single mothering? The literature seems to show that many women who were deprived of strong family ties, often beginning with a live-in dad, sorely miss those ties. They seek to form them with the young males in their lives. In poorer communities,

---

9   See sources cited at note 1, *supra*.

10   John Cacioppo and William Patrick, *Loneliness: Human Nature and the Need for Social Connection* (New York: W.W. Norton & Co., 2008).

these young men, too, have often lacked a steady father figure in their lives. Neither the men nor the women see much marriage in such communities and so have few or no models for how to be successfully married. For the woman, a baby, unlike a boyfriend, will possibly be hers in a special way her entire life. Maybe, she hopes, it will tie the father to her and seal the relationship in a more secure way. But this doesn't usually work out, even if she is cohabiting with the father at the time of the birth.

Having a baby also grants the young woman entry into the community of young mothers with babies who live in her neighborhood or go to her school. It is a bond. The young mothers then share the same worries and joys, membership in the same government outreach and welfare programs, and something much more. They have attained a role in the community that can garner a certain kind of respect: a role as one who gives, one who loves, one who sacrifices for a child and who "takes care." It is a kind of badge of maturity, a place in the world, a role with its own heroism, in contrast to many other roles that seem out of reach to her, such as the roles of wife, college-educated woman, or working woman with an interesting job.

What about the more privileged woman or girl? Certainly, in today's world and economy, and with today's continuing high rates of divorce and nonmarital parenting generally, she too might be responding to the desire for human communion and an adult role in this world as one who takes care of others. She too might be responding to the lack of other futures she can genuinely envisage and hope to pursue. But in her case, another strong factor is likely at work, a factor that certainly also affects poor women, but which might be the most pressing for women with more economic and educational advantages: the pressures operating in the current sex and mating markets.[11] What I mean is this: The cycle between the easy availability of both contraception and abortion and the changing social mores about sex results in more pressure than ever before for a young woman who wants the interest of men to agree to engage in sexual intercourse even without any personal relationship commitment. Sociologists, psychologists, and law and economic scholars have confirmed this phenomenon again and again.[12] Take the baby out of sex (as contraception and abortion permit), and sex is suddenly much less of a big deal for those without well-formed understandings of its emotional and spiritual significance or of its impact on society.

And as more women perceive sex to be less risky and agree to nonmarital or even, in the new and depressing scholarly term "nonrelationship" sex (sex without a prior personal attachment), it simply happens that there are more nonmarital pregnancies and more nonmarital births and even more abortions. Scholars call this phenomenon "risk compensation." (As when, for example, more people speed after seatbelt laws go into effect.) As more women agree to these sexual relationships, there is increased pressure toward nonmarital sex upon those women who would previously have resisted it. In fact, in the past, they resisted in some part because their female peers would surely have socially punished them. But as more women move over to the "new norm," wider social

11   See Elise Italiano, "Sex, Mating, and the Marriage 'Market,'" Chapter 3 in this book.

12   See *e.g.* George A. Akerlof, Janet L Yellen, and Michael L. Katz, "An Analysis of Out-of-Wedlock Childbearing in the United States," *Quarterly Journal of Economics 111* (1996): 277. Timothy Reichert, "Bitter Pill," *First Things* (May 2010), 25.

norms begin to change. Women don't "punish" other women socially any longer for transgressing chastity, nor do men. We may not have thought about this phenomenon among women in ordinary communities all over the United States, but we have almost certainly seen it among elites in the entertainment, media, academic, and political worlds; their "new norm" has been brought to bear on every town in America with a TV and an Internet connection.

So now that we have a clue as to the *why* part of the equation, what might we do, practically speaking, as citizens, as women, and as a Church, to assist women caught in this dilemma? My proposal is next.

Acknowledge the Longing for Communion, but Talk Straight

Today, the government is the leading voice of anything resembling a widespread cautionary message about nonmarital births. But the government is doing a pretty lousy job of it, in my view, which means (as the Church already knew) that the Church is an even more necessary player than anyone thought. We have a better grasp of human nature in connection with sexuality, and we also have a vast network of people and institutions qualified and practically situated to make a strong effort.

Preliminarily, I would note government's communication failures. First, both state and federal governments speak almost exclusively to teens, yet teens account for only 17 percent of all nonmarital births. Women twenty and over make up the rest. But in respect to this older group, government has adopted the message: "Sexual expression is a completely private matter, as well as morally neutral as long as you get what you desire, whether this means a baby or no baby, and no disease." But sex outside of marriage is neither morally nor socially neutral — even consensual sex between adults. We know too much about its effects — on vulnerable women, on the relations between women and men, on the well-being of children, and even on the economy as a whole — to deal in such rubbish any longer.

Second, a review of government-sponsored literature regarding the meaning of human sexuality reveals this: It focuses primarily on the relationship between avoiding pregnancy and maximizing the potential of the lone individual. It fails completely to account for the human desire to form communion with another human person and to become a giver, as part of the normal course of human development and maturity. In so failing, the government never even broaches the subject of one of the important drivers of behavior: Men and women nearing or beginning adulthood aspire to love and to give. Each wants to be more than a self-maximizing individual avoiding a relationship with another person who might ask something of them.

Third, the government has never acknowledged the phenomenon of "risk compensation" in increasing rates of non-marital pregnancies and abortions over the same time period that the government has increased funding for birth-control programs — and sometimes abortion services, too.

Fourth, the government has refused to robustly sing the praises of healthy marriage to the extent that it should, beginning when children are young. And, finally, at the federal level, it is even undermining the "marriage-children" connection, by claiming currently that it sees no important difference between unions where procreation is possible (opposite sex) and where it is not (same sex).

Clearly then, the ball is in the Church's court. The Catholic Church has an impressive couple of thousand years of reflection upon human sexuality. Our last two popes in particular have expended enormous intellectual and pastoral energies promoting the Church's beautiful "yes" to sex: sex as an expression of human communion and sharing in God's image, and sex as an invitation to share in God's creative power. This is most comprehensively collected in the teachings known as the "Theology of the Body," Blessed John Paul II's first 130 "Wednesday lectures" from 1978 to 1982. These focus on the meaning of the human body as a perspective for understanding the meaning of life, including the meaning of love in all its aspects.[13]

Yet while the Church's teachings offer the promise of real help, especially to younger women and men, they are not yet sufficiently deployed. And as already noted, there is also the problem of the potential for confusion as observers see both the Church's strong disapproval of nonmarital sex alongside its obvious welcome of new human life, no matter the circumstances. Let me start by responding to the potential for a much better effort at communicating the Church's teachings.

It is only quite recently that a larger number of dioceses, parishes, and national Catholic groups are speaking heart-to-heart and mind-to-mind with younger women and men in their teens and twenties about the realities of relationships today, the meaning of sexual intercourse, and the links between current social and psychological research and Catholic teach-

---

13   Blessed John Paul II, *Man And Woman He Created Them: A Theology of the Body* (Michael Waldstein, trans.)(Boston: Pauline Books, 2006).

ing. It is surprising and sad that it has taken the Church so long to begin communicating this message to a wider audience, given the amount of wisdom the Church has on the anthropology (the "nature") of the human person, especially where romantic relationships are concerned. The Church's slow response is also troubling because of the opportunity offered by today's dovetailing of religious and scientific sources and because of the good of women and men and the flourishing that might result from an enthusiastic and realistic engagement with this kind of material. Practically speaking too (also noted briefly above), there is the opportunity offered by the network of Catholic parishes, schools, hospitals, and social services reaching out to Americans of every background in every state.

The Church has much to offer about where to find meaning in sex and in male-female relationships, but it is too little shouted from the housetops. The good news about this situation? There is a lot of room for improvement. The bad news? Several generations have grown up and reared their own children without the benefit of the Church's credible and inspiring teachings in this area.

What about the potential for confusion should the Church speak out a great deal more? What might that confusion look like? At the very same time she is raining warnings upon adolescent and young-adult women about cohabitation and single parenting, the Catholic Church, other churches, and the pro-life movement are saying to this same audience:

> Should you find yourself pregnant, allow us to appeal to your hearts. You know this pregnancy we warned you about? Well, now that it's here, open your heart, your mind, your wallet, and all of your remaining years to it. Because this is an

innocent child we're dealing with here. Become the loving mother who not only has the last word regarding this child's continued existence, but who also might affect the course of his entire life. Fear not. You can draw on the enormous web of private support that the Catholic community and other religious communities and the pro-life movement are able to provide.

Are these two sets of messages — "don't do it" and "if you're pregnant, go the distance" — the best way to speak to single parenting? Should we be saying something more or different? As women? As a Church? What might be most helpful to the single woman? And the children some will inevitably have? These are challenging questions, and though I do not pretend to have the only or best answer, I do have something to offer. I offer it knowing the ridicule it might bring us, or the charges that we are totally out of step when it comes to sex, or that we are throwing women back to the 1950s, or that we are, regarding sex (in Pope Benedict's words), "turn[ing] to bitterness the most precious thing in life ... blow[ing] the whistle just when the joy which is the Creator's gift offers us a happiness which is itself a certain foretaste of the Divine."[14] It is this: never to forget the baby when we are dealing with sex. In the inimitable words of author Jennifer Fulwiler, who opened my head to this, there is a world of difference between the culture's message that "unprotected sex makes babies" and our message that "sex makes babies."[15]

---

14   Pope Benedict XVI, *Deus Caritas Est*, encyclical letter (www.vatican.va, 2005), 3.

15   Jennifer Fulwiler, "A Sexual Revolution: From Pro-Choice Atheist to Pro-Life Catholic," *America*, July 7, 2008.

The former message casts babies as failures of technology and will. The latter, however, opens up a world of positive reflections. To wit: God could have "put" procreation anywhere he wanted. He could have brought new human life into the world in any fashion whatsoever, utterly disconnected from any union between men and women. But he didn't. He put it in the loving embrace of the man and the woman. He put it in the act that every race and nation throughout history associates with the communication of love and (still often) commitment between one man and one woman. And he made that baby's flourishing dependent upon the continuing care and affection of that man and that woman together. Yes, sex also makes for bonding between men and women. Sex makes for personal happiness and pleasure and a sense of well-being. All true, all good, and even wonderful. But more stunningly, if you will, more who-but-God-could-have-arranged-this? — sex makes babies. Re-educating, re-evangelizing, re-emphasizing this point is crucial. It is the very polar opposite of the world's message today, which makes it all the more daunting. But I have come to believe it is the beginning of a real answer.

Interestingly, you will note that this statement is not a judgment of the single mother, or about males versus females; it is just a fact that is true, and that all should recognize. Within it are contained respect for the vulnerable child, awe at God's design, and many clues about why society has always linked marriage with sex with babies, in that order. It doesn't obscure either the Church's love for babies or her assistance to their mothers, nor does it obscure the norm: save sex for marriage. It confirms all of these. I say this knowing how out of the times it appears to render me, not to mention the Church. But I propose it because I believe it to be true, based not first on religious doctrine, but on the evidence all around us in the world. On the evidence of what makes women and men happy and healthy, and what makes children secure and society stable. In addition, I propose it because Catholic teachings — Scripture, theology, pastoral reflections — confirm this evidence with profound insights into human nature and human love, managing not only to inform us, but to inspire. If ever there was a confluence of evidence that should spur us to action, this is it.

Chapter 10

Beyond Politics
Everyday Catholic Life

Kim Daniels, J.D.

 We've all been there. The block party where your neighbor sees you putting ketchup on your hamburger and decides this is the time to ask you why Catholics won't let women be priests. Or the family vacation where, as you reach bleary-eyed for coffee, your uncle looks up from his morning paper and asks why the bishops can't just stick to things they know and keep their noses out of economics. Or the night out with friends, where somehow the fact that you're pro-life comes up; all of a sudden you're in a serious, uncomfortable discussion instead of talking about weekend plans over drinks.

These days being Catholic often seems to mean playing Defender of the Faith at a moment's notice, ready with answers on hot-button issues for every disgruntled uncle or curious neighbor. And that's great. These moments are everyday opportunities to witness to our faith, chances for others to hear why the Church teaches what it does, and to connect those teachings with a friendly face.

But let's be honest: Sometimes we just want to have a cup of coffee. More importantly, it can be frustrating when others seem to reduce our faith to its positions on controversial political and social issues. We know Catholicism is more than that, and we want others to know that as well. And we have a sense that others used to see Catholicism as something more than controversy. It's hard to imagine our grandmothers spending any time at all explaining the male priesthood to their Protestant neighbors.

Of course, some of our grandmothers didn't have many Protestant neighbors. And that's part of the difference: Just a few generations ago, American Catholics often inhabited not only thickly Catholic neighborhoods but a deeply Catholic culture. And by that I don't just mean that *The Bells of St. Mary's* played at the local theater, or that Fulton Sheen held forth on television.

Culture is much more than pop culture. But it's also much more than high culture, more than art, literature, and music. It's shared habits and understandings and affections rooted in a particular place. It gives a particular shape to family, to friendship, and to daily living. A vibrant culture is reflected in an everyday life interwoven with something beyond the everyday, something holy.

Not too long ago, many American Catholics inhabited just such a culture, one in which their faith suffused their lives. It informed where they lived; it informed what they ate; it informed where their kids went to school and the sports teams they joined and what they did for fun. For better and for worse, Catholicism was the air that many American Catholics breathed.

That's not the world most of us live in today. Today the air we breathe is thinner. For a host of complicated reasons, the everyday lives of many American Catholics are no longer particularly distinctive from the everyday lives of members of other faiths. And so non-Catholics can be forgiven for reducing our faith to its positions on hot-button issues, for often that's all that seems to distinguish us from anyone else.

But we know it's more than that. Our faith should be part of the air we breathe. Making that happen — building a Catholic culture in our homes, among our friends, in our parishes — is the most important task facing Catholic women today. It's got nothing to do with *The Bells of St. Mary's* and everything to do with weaving joy and love into the particular circumstances of our everyday lives, whatever their challenges. The question is how we get from here to there in a way that fits our time and place.

Everyday Faith

My first exposure to an everyday Catholic culture happened on a high school trip to Ireland in the mid-1980s. Soon after our arrival I saw something very simple that's stayed with me ever since. As we walked in front of a Catholic church, a man walking next to us ... crossed himself. In public. While hurrying down the sidewalk. Without a hint of self-consciousness.

I did a double take. Had anyone else noticed this? Why did he do that? Was there something particularly special about that church? Apparently not, because soon I began to notice things like this happening again and again. A woman saying the Rosary as she walked along a country lane. An old man tipping his hat in the general direction of the tabernacle as he walked past a church. A picture of the Sacred Heart tacked on the wall in a pub.

What was so remarkable about all this was how unremarkable it was. These people weren't trying to prove how holy they were. They weren't making any particular effort to live their faith in the world. They were just doing what came naturally in their time and place, and at that time and in that place outward expressions of Catholicism came naturally.

To a suburban American kid, that naturalness was striking. It showed me a small glimpse of what it meant to live in a Catholic place. It helped me understand that these small acts of everyday piety witnessed to a deeper faith, a faith that I happily shared, a faith I now wanted to learn more about.

Now let's not romanticize things: I also remember eating a lot of cold sausage and gummy oatmeal on that trip and spending many afternoons wondering if we would ever stop walking. Thatched roofs and freckle-faced kids don't mean everything's rosy. And, of course, we shouldn't sentimentalize mid-century Catholic America either; not everyone had big Sunday dinners cooked by their Italian grandmothers, and we don't need another *New York Times* columnist to tell us that those Sunday dinners could be stifling, or lead to years of dieting struggles, or whatever.

But these cultures reflected, however dimly, that Catholics believed that the good and the true and the beautiful existed just beyond the everyday world — and sometimes overflowed into it. They reflected a living faith of feasting and fasting, joy and grief, generosity and sacrifice that witnessed to the truths of our faith without having to articulate them.

In the World, but Not of It

It's often hard to find reflections of the good and the true and the beautiful in the culture that surrounds us today. Its problems are familiar: an unthinking consumerism taught by ads that tell kids they need the new Lego Captain America Avenging Cycle, or that tell twentysomething women that this year's "summer must-haves" are fundamentally different from the ones in the back of her closet from last year. A routine coarseness emanating from the screens we view. A loss of a sense of place, of stability, of home. A casual acceptance of each new technology that comes along, even though they too often make our lives more frenetic and distracted.

I won't belabor these familiar problems; it's dispiriting to rehearse them again and again. We know the larger challenges our generation faces. Our job is to respond to them in our own lives. For the most part, that's a cultural — not political — task. It requires not legislation, but everyday efforts to work with those closest to us to build this essential ability to respond in ways that help the common good.

Catholics bring particularly useful resources to the challenge of pushing back against a culture that, to paraphrase Catholic Worker cofounder Peter Maurin, doesn't make it "easy to be good."[1] We need to reclaim those resources. As Catholics we know, for instance, that our faith calls us to be in the world, even as we're not to be of the world. This means that most of us should resist the temptation to retreat from society, to go off on our own to try to create a purer, more holy community. Christians in other times and places have faced cultures much more hostile than ours — sometimes even died for their faith — yet still managed to "shine like stars in the world" (Phil 2:15).

We need to do the same. Pope Benedict XVI speaks of Catholics today forming a "creative minority" in society, en-

---

gaging culture while remaining true to our faith.[2] Engaging a culture does not mean embracing it, of course; it means countering its values with our own. To engage the culture on the ground, where we live, means countering materialism with simplicity; transience with rootedness; and coarseness with self-giving love. It means living lives of sacrifice and generosity, integrity and joy, and in doing so, quietly witnessing to our faith.

Recently a woman in our parish passed away. She and her husband of sixty-two years had been members of our parish for more than fifty years. They had nine children and twenty-three grandchildren. Their children had gone to our parish school, and a number of their grandchildren had as well; some are still there. She was as much a part of our parish and its history as it is possible to be. And, of course, these bare facts don't tell the whole story. Just to see her and her husband at Mass on Sunday — always with smiles on their faces, always surrounded by whatever family happened to be there that day — told anyone with eyes to see what a well-lived Catholic life looks like. It looks generous and self-sacrificing, and joyful.

I doubt this wonderful woman thought of herself as a "creative minority," but I have no doubt that she was. She didn't assimilate to the rapidly changing culture around her; she engaged it, just by building a life, and a family, that served as a light for others, and doing that in a positive way. And let me tell you, her funeral was standing-room only, and there wasn't a dry eye in the house.

She did something else that was profoundly countercultural, and also particularly Catholic: She rooted her life in a

---

2   Sandro Magister, "Interview with Pope Benedict: De-Christianized Europe. Church as a 'Creative Minority,'" *Catholic Online* (October 2, 2009), www.catholic .org/international/international_story.php?id=34545, accessed June 1, 2012.

particular place, and she stayed there. By committing to a parish, she and others like her helped build a robust community that people can count on. They can count on a thriving school to educate their kids; they can count on a place to serve others in their own neighborhood; they can count on the possibility of true and long-lasting friendships in an increasingly transient and dislocated place. Because parishes by their nature root the sacred in the everyday — because the holy sacrifice of the Mass takes place right after the school bell rings, and right before the bazaar gets planned in the basement — holiness becomes a visible part of daily life.

One of the surest steps to rebuilding Catholic culture would be for Catholics to commit themselves to their local parishes when possible; to resist the urge to "church-shop"; to think of what they're giving up before they move to that bigger house a few zip codes away. Everyone who stays put is doing something to build a robust, living place, a place where faces become familiar enough to be approachable and then approachable enough to be friends.

In such parishes people take care of each other. They know, without extra effort, when there's sickness in a family, or when someone's kid is having trouble, or when another person's baby has finally arrived. And more often than not someone does the right thing — drops off a meal on a doorstep; lingers in the hallway just to talk; is simply present for others. After all, we're not meant to be Catholics alone; we're meant to be Catholics together. We're meant to love God and our neighbor — together.

And in this time, and in this culture, being Catholic together should more often mean sticking with particular people, in a particular place, so that we come to share memories and stories and sorrows and joys, and thus become more what we were meant to be — a "people set apart" for holiness. That holiness is no less important for happening on doorsteps and in hallways, and it's the essential thread in any living culture.

"Women's Work"

The responsibility of building such vibrant, rooted cultures more often than not falls to women. I don't mean that all women are called to live primarily domestic lives, of course; there are as many vocations as there are women. Some vocations center on marriage and children, some center on friends and extended family. Some women stay home to raise their kids, and some pursue full-time professional work. Some women work part time, or from home, or part time from home. But whatever their vocation, women very often know in their hearts that people are hungry for community. And that's what building culture is all about: creating the circumstances in which real community — thick with memory and friendship and faith — can thrive. Women often have a particular gift for building culture so understood.

Recognizing that women have many different vocations doesn't mean giving short shrift to one particular vocation: motherhood. The idea of motherhood is central to our faith; the fact of motherhood is central to many of our lives. And it is often primarily through their mother's efforts that children first encounter the beginnings of a faith-filled, other-centered culture, the "domestic church" of the family.

There, children first learn the virtues that make life in community livable — forgiveness, patience, charity (at least until someone steals the last brownie). They learn about order and beauty (at least until the laundry piles up). And they learn about goodness (at least as the opposite of badness). However imperfectly, we begin to build real culture in our homes — and thus the larger world — whenever we orient our families toward God.

And when the laundry is piled up, and the kids are fighting over who stole what, that is when women are most grateful for friendship. Friendship might not seem like something particularly Catholic or cultural, but bear with me for a second. Notice how often Jesus acts as a friend in the Gospels: He eats, drinks, and celebrates with his disciples; he shares his thoughts with them and challenges them; he asks for their help. He no longer calls them servants, but friends, for "I have made known to you everything that I have heard from my Father" (Jn 15:15). Friendship is central to Jesus's life on earth, and it's central to our faith.

It's also central to culture. Building culture is about building true communities, and communities are made up of friends. Building those friendships takes work — but it's fun work. The Christian "duty of hospitality" can mean many things, but one thing it means is getting to know others; inviting them into your home and sharing a meal and being together. That's about the easiest duty I know. And how attractive our local Catholic cultures would be — how effective our witness — if we tried to live this ideal of friendship; if we showed the world, in writer Hilaire Belloc's words, that "wherever the Catholic sun does shine / There's always laughter and good red wine."[3]

---

3 Hilaire Belloc, "The Catholic Sun," www.poemhunter.com/poem/the-catholic-sun-2/, accessed June 4, 2012.

More than the words we say or the views we hold, it's how we live together that builds culture in our families, among our friends, and in our parishes. Blessed John Paul II recognized the fundamental importance of building culture, and the centrality of families and friendships to that project. He also wrote, moreover, of our responsibility to spread the Good News to those around us; to let them know that "no one is without a family in this world: the Church is a home and family for everyone, especially those who 'labor and are heavy laden.'"[4]

This is the witness that a renewed and rooted Catholic culture of faith, family, and friendship can give to the exhausted culture from which it springs. It's no stretch to say that women must take the lead in this great project — family to family, friend to friend, in parishes across the country. This everyday task of building culture from the ground up is not something routine, or incidental, or secondary. It's beautiful and radical and essential, and it's up to Catholic women to help it take root.

Kim Daniels is a mother of six, a lawyer, and coordinator of Catholic Voices USA.

---

4   Blessed John Paul II, *Familiaris Consortio*, apostolic exhortation (1981), 85.

Afterword

Helen M. Alvaré

It is impossible to synthesize all that has gone on in this book. It would not be a useful project either. Each chapter is such an interplay of the author's unique life, Catholic teachings, and the challenges thrown down by our modern American environment that it would be difficult — and reductive — merely to summarize them. But if there isn't one thesis here, there is perhaps one inspiration, one call to action. It is this: You are not alone, so be not afraid.

Blessed John Paul II could not have realized how directly he was speaking to women when he offered this same phrase — "Be not afraid" — to inaugurate his pontificate in 1978. He could not know how fervently women would embrace his later, explicit invitation to fashion a "new feminism." But he was prophetic all the same: It would take more than a little courage to wade into the sometimes chaotic debates raging in American society about the nature and roles of women.

By the 1970s, many of the frenzied attempts to define feminism for women were already bearing ugly weeds alongside healthy crops. There was talk about opportunity without corresponding consideration of responsibility. There was positive talk about work outside the home, but almost none about family. There was talk about equality, but not about what equality would look like in the context of a two-sexed and complementary humanity. And there was talk of a sexual revolution without understanding human nature and the body-soul connection as necessary elements of any such talk.

Stunningly, debates about women still operate largely according to these seriously flawed dynamics. Consequently, ideas, practices, and doctrines associated with the Catholic faith and intellectual tradition — whether about loving service as the meaning of life, or about opposite-sex complementarity, body-soul integrity, and the importance of the organic family — still, and often, find themselves on the receiving end of verbal firing squads. Firing squads composed of influential people — politicians, media figures, entertainers, or even seemingly expert academics. It's tough to endure if you are a woman who feels moved to "give an explanation ... for your hope" (1 Pt 3:15, NAB). In this environment, "be not afraid" is not only a good place to start, but a necessary part of a toolkit for daily living.

I say this from my own experience, too. A good deal of the time, the criticism or even dismissal I experience as a mouthy and sometimes "public" Catholic female simply pings off some invisible barrier I have been gifted. But occasionally I grow tired or embarrassed for my family in reaction to nasty headlines or claims that I play fast and loose with the truth, or that I am simply a brainless mouthpiece for an all-male celibate hierarchy. What would it feel like, I wonder, not to be the perennial barbarian-at-the-cocktail-party?

Yet I'm not genuinely tempted to find out. Because the stronger pull is toward integrity, toward imitating lives like those of my coauthors here, lives that are turned toward God. The path my coauthors have described, in their varied ways, often began with dissatisfaction with the world's proposed answers to women's deepest questions. Those answers were closed off from the transcendent, from God. My coauthors and I realized, rather, that when we let God in, better answers suggested themselves, answers that satisfied both our souls and our minds. Consequently, we have learned not only to give God time to speak to us in prayer, but to listen to what he tells us in our conversations with one another.

This does not mean we cease our intellectual exploration, or that we fail to learn from experience. On the contrary, God is the God of reason, too, and intends us to integrate faith and reason, allowing each of these sources to shed light upon the other. We gain wisdom and peace too when we keep reading, keep thinking, keep analyzing, and keep sizing up our reflections and conclusions against the best opposing arguments we encounter.

At the same time, it is good to keep in mind, as Pope Benedict XVI says, that the human being is above all the object of a call to love, not of an accusation. God did not create us to be fighting machines, to be miserable, to see only the negative, or to hate the world and those who disagree with us. He created us rather to be givers and receivers of love. We are first and foremost to delight in all the good gifts he provides, including in particular the gift of those other human beings, those "neighbors" who will — despite outward appearances — need our help, even our love, at some time or another. At the very least, we need to "give them the look of love which they crave" (*Deus Caritas Est*, 18). When we "give first" — like God in whose image we are made — then we can never be devastated, or left with nothing, or left alone. Rather, we feel ourselves to be happier and more in harmony not only with God, but also with our fellow human beings.

Intellectually and as a matter of faith these are conclusions you probably already accept. But I hope this book will help you see how they actually play out in the experience of Catholic women of many backgrounds and occupations — Catholic women not so different from you. I hope you will feel supported on your own path toward answering some of the thorniest questions facing women, and the Church, and society today. I hope you will feel stronger and more secure not only in your faith and in your reason, but also in your God-given capacity to "speak for yourself" when the moment arrives.

Acknowledgments

I would like to thank my coauthors for their talent, their ability to think about hard (not to mention often controversial) topics, their willingness to work under truly demanding deadlines, and their patience with the editing process. It was a privilege to work with women whose intelligence and goodness can so readily inspire others.

Thanks also to Cindy Cavnar, my editor at Our Sunday Visitor. For decades, I have read authors' thanking their editors and have wondered at the vehemence of their words. Now I understand. But for her dogged work ethic, her ability to combine praise and exhortation in perfect amounts, and her gifts of speech and judgment, this book would not have been completed.

Thanks finally to my husband and children, whose love and forbearance and wit make every day possible, and fun.